SCILLY¹
ARCHAEOLOGICA

Jeanette Ratcliff
Cornwall Archaeological Unit
Cornwall County Council

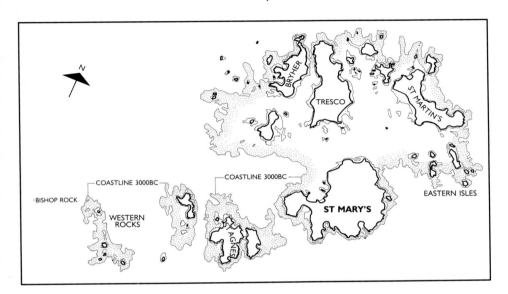

THE ARCHAEOLOGY of Scilly has attracted continuous interest since the mid-eighteenth century, when it was recorded by the famous Cornish antiquarian, William Borlase. More than a thousand archaeological sites represent over four thousand years of occupation, from prehistory to World War Two.

Though Scilly is generally culturally similar to West Cornwall, from where it was originally settled, its insular character has always been an important factor in its development. During prehistory relative isolation led to the intensification of certain traditions, for example the unique concentration of Bronze Age entrance graves. From Roman times, however, long distance trade brought Scilly into the wider world, and during the post-medieval period it became strategically important in the defence of England, being successively fortified over almost three hundred and fifty years.

An unusual aspect of Scilly's archaeology is the presence of remains below high water, the result of low lying land being submerged by a gradual rise in sea level.

Although coastal erosion and, to a lesser extent, modern development, tourism and agriculture are continuing threats, most surviving monuments are remarkably well preserved — being largely constructed of granite, and lying mostly on uninhabited islands or areas of moorland not intensively used since the Bronze Age. These downs and clifftops are generally well served by footpaths and covered by low heather or grass, making them very accessible to the public. This book provides an up-to-date summary of the archaeology and history of Scilly and brief descriptions of the best monuments to visit island by island.

Sites mentioned in the text which appear in the gazetteer are referenced by their site number shown thus: [73]

A SUBMERGED LANDSCAPE

TODAY the Isles of Scilly comprise two hundred individual rocks and islands, but ten thousand years ago, at the end of the last ice age, the picture was very different. Current thinking suggests that the archipelago may have consisted of a single land mass stretching from the Western Rocks to the Eastern Isles and from Peninnis to Shipman Head. As the ice sheets melted the sea level rose, and by 3000BC submergence of low lying areas had led to the formation of a number of separate islands. The main one encompassed the modern islands of St Mary's, Bryher, Tresco and St Martin's, while St Agnes, Annet and the Western Rocks constituted three smaller tracts of land. (*See the map on the previous page*) Throughout later prehistory the sea continued to rise, but it was probably not until the end of the Roman period that today's islands began to appear. Even as late as the eleventh century AD most of these would have been joined at low water.

This model for the submergence of Scilly is based on a sea level rise of 2.1-2.6 millimetres per year, calculated by using the vertical position of dated submerged archaeological remains, and assuming that they were originally sited just above the shoreline. The distribution of Cornish and English coastal placenames supports the theory that the formation of modern day Scilly was not complete until the early Tudor period. Pre-16th century Cornish placenames are found around the outer edges of the Islands; later, English names keep to the inward facing shores.

Marine inundation may also have resulted from tidal surges (exceptional storm tides). Whilst exact details of the submergence are unclear, its undoubted occurrence is indicated by the prehistoric (and later) sites lying between high and low water. These are the remains of houses, field walls and graves, the best examples being on Samson Flats [59], in Green Bay (Bryher) [8], West Porth (Tean) [62], and on either side of Carn Near (Tresco) [64 and 65]. In recent years winter storms have exposed intertidal peat deposits. Dating of these can reveal when they were formed and when they were overwhelmed by the sea. The pollen they contain will give an idea of the contemporary surrounding vegetation.

Analysis of peat samples from the two major wetlands of Higher and Lower Moors on St Mary's has provided a general vegetational history for Scilly. During the 6th millennium BC the Islands were predominantly covered by oak woodland, with hazel understorey and patches of elm and ash. Birch formed scrub in exposed coastal localities or as an understorey to the oak woodland. Around 3000 BC there is evidence for the partial clearance of woodland for cultivation. However, this is followed by a period of forest regeneration, when birch trees became more abundant than before. Oak also occurred, but hazel declined. The presence of cereal and herbaceous pollen indicates that some land remained open. At around 2500 BC there was a marked decline in woodland, with herbaceous flora predominant, indicating an open and pastoral landscape. Evidence from early settlement sites confirms this general picture of a deciduous forest which by the Iron Age, at least, had become largely transformed into an open environment of cultivated fields, pasture and heathland, not dissimilar to the landscape of today.

Early Visitors
8000BC–4000BC MESOLITHIC PERIOD

FROM THE end of the last Ice Age until the development of farming, Southern Britain was occupied by bands of semi-nomadic peoples; who lived by gathering vegetable foods, hunting wild animals and harvesting the resources of the sea. The evidence for gatherer-hunters in Scilly is sparse, in part because they made temporary shelters out of animal hide and used materials such as skin, gut, bone, wood, vegetable fibre and stone to make their tools and equipment. All but the stone are perishable and leave little trace. In addition, camps would probably have been concentrated around the coastline which is now submerged. Existing archaeological evidence is restricted to a dozen worked flints and the pollen sequence from the Higher Moors peat deposit. Most of the flints are tiny microliths, used as points or barbs on arrows, spears and harpoons, but one is a sharpening flake from an axe. The only flint working site identified is at Old Quay, St Martin's. At Higher Moors, the presence of birch pollen in the earliest vegetational phase is probably due to mesolithic activity; initial disturbance of the virgin forest by burning to flush out game and encourage the growth of lush pasture. The larger land mass, with its plains and sheltered slopes covered in mixed oak woodland could have supported substantial numbers of large mammals (such as red deer), smaller animals and birds, and must have provided an abundance of plant foods (roots, fungi, berries, nuts and fruits). An extensive coastline with sheltered inlets, sandy flats and outlying rocks would have ensured a plentiful supply of fish, seals, shellfish and edible seaweeds.

Pioneer Farmers
4000BC–2500BC NEOLITHIC PERIOD

BY THE NEOLITHIC, people in Southern Britain were already beginning to manage their environment. Between 4000 and 3500 BC increased domestication of animals and the deliberate cultivation of food-plants marked the advent of farming. Gathering, hunting and fishing continued to play an important role, but the introduction of agriculture restricted movement and led to the establishment of more permanent settlements and the evolution of complex social and political groupings. Large stone (megalithic) monuments were constructed as ritual foci and territorial markers, and tribal centres developed. Pottery-making skills were developed, there were improvements in the techniques of working flint and other types of stone, and prestige objects (especially stone axes) were traded over a wide area.

In Scilly the pollen evidence shows partial forest clearance and cultivation of cereal crops around 3000 BC, but this was followed by a period of woodland regeneration and apparent agricultural decline. The only identified neolithic artefacts are a handful of stone axes and flint arrowheads, a flint adze and a few sherds of middle-neolithic pottery. The pottery came from Bant's Carn entrance grave and from a series of pits excavated in East Porth, Samson. No other neolithic settlements or ceremonial monuments have been identified, but the submergence will have destroyed any low lying and coastal sites, and since most surviving prehistoric houses and entrance graves are unexcavated some of these may have their origins in this period. However, present evidence suggests that Scilly was not permanently settled until the Bronze Age and that the few neolithic artefacts found represent occupation of a more temporary nature.

The First Settlers
2500BC–700BC BRONZE AGE

IN CONTRAST, there are a remarkable number of Bronze Age monuments in Scilly. At the beginning of this period the Islands were permanently settled from West Cornwall and farming began on a large scale.

Occupation debris from settlements reveals that their inhabitants practised a mixed subsistence economy; as well as growing crops and raising stock, they fished, gathered shellfish and hunted wild animals and birds. Cereals such as naked barley and emmer wheat were cultivated, with pulses such as the celtic, horse and horn bean. Domesticated animals included dwarf breeds of ox and sheep, and a very small pig with large feet, probably still semi-wild. Fish were a major source of protein, preserved by wind drying or salting using evaporated brine. Species caught include pollack, conger, ling, turbot, wrasse, bass, plaice, cod, saithe, sea-bream, gurnard and gilthead; probably mainly caught on lines from the shore or from small boats. Shellfish were used for bait and food, and the shells for decoration. Limpet shells usually make up the bulk of Bronze Age middens (domestic rubbish heaps). Also collected were cockles, dog-whelks, strand shells, thick topshells, snails and great scallops (useful as lamps). Birds were important for their meat, feathers and oil, and identified species include guillemot, razorbill, raven, goose, gannet, white stork, and possibly swan. Amongst the wild mammals hunted were red deer, horse, pig, seal and dolphin. Whale meat was consumed when carcasses were washed ashore, their blubber and that of seals being melted down to provide oil for lamps.

The houses they lit were round, built of thick double-faced stone walling and had conical roofs thatched with ferns, reeds or straw. There are over one hundred and forty of these houses and whilst many are probably Bronze Age only fifteen can be dated to this period. Settlements favoured low-lying land and many will have been submerged or destroyed by the sea. Most surviving houses

are simple structures, but a few have annexes and additional rooms. They usually occur in pairs or small groups, sometimes interconnected. On the whole, the evidence suggests people were living in family groups or hamlets rather than villages. Internal diameters of buildings range from 2.5-13.0 metres, presumably reflecting variation in the number of occupants and the function of the building (some must have been barns or byres rather than dwelling houses). Usually there is a single entrance flanked by stone door jambs, but no window openings. Floors are formed by subsoil (ram), but stone paving is sometimes found, especially around entrances and the inside of walls. Other internal features are clay and stone-lined hearths (often centrally placed); stone-lined drains; post-holes and post-hole stones (for holding roof supports); door pivot-stones; stone benches and internal partitions (sometimes forming a radial pattern). Corn-drying ovens and clay or stone-lined pits (probably for storing water) have also been found.

These early settlements invariably lie within or adjacent to the remains of contemporary field systems; small rectilinear fields defined by boulder walls, stony banks (the result of field clearance) and lynchets (terraces formed by ploughsoil collecting against the downhill side of the field). As with unexcavated houses, it is difficult to precisely date these systems, but those lying on exposed moorlands — like Shipman Head Down [13], Castle Down [68] and Chapel Down [28] — must have been laid out before the present unworkable peaty soils developed. Submerged field walls may also be of early origin, but probably continued in use throughout prehistory and, in some cases, into the Roman and early medieval periods.

On the edge of these field systems and beyond, on hilltops, ridges and coastal plateaux, Bronze Age people built their ceremonial monuments. Most impressive are the entrance graves. Over eighty have been recorded. These are part of a late Neolithic

Entrance grave at Innisidgen Carn, St Mary's

tradition originating in West Cornwall, which continued for much longer in Scilly, possibly until 700 BC. They consist of a roughly circular stone and earth cairn, usually revetted by a stone kerb (or kerbs) and containing a rectangular chamber constructed of slabs or coursed walling, covered by several large capstones and, in a few cases, entered via an uncovered passage. Both cairn and chamber often incorporate natural boulders and outcrops, which adds to their megalithic appearance. Their size varies considerably, from 3.5-25.0 metres in diameter and 0.3-2.5 metres in height, and this may reflect the

Early field walls on Shipman Head Down

differing social status of the people using them and/or the different functions of the monuments themselves. The majority occur in pairs or small groups, although isolated examples are not uncommon. There are also two larger groupings: on North Hill, Samson [58] and Porth Hellick Down, St Mary's [51]. Judging from human remains found in excavated chambers, burial was one of their main functions. Cremation was usual, with burnt bones deposited loose or in urns and sometimes accompanied by grave goods such as bronze objects, bone points, hammerstones, pumice, and glass or faience beads. In three chambers successive deposits representing a large number of individuals (sixty plus at Knackyboy Cairn, St Martins) were made over several hundred years. However, entrance graves probably fulfilled much wider social and ritual functions, for example as territorial markers and places where offerings were made to ensure the fertility of the land and a good harvest. The latter interpretation is suggested by the fact that many have a direct relationship with early field boundaries and several had deposits of settlement debris, humic material and, in one case, a saddle quern on their chamber floors.

Rarer and even more enigmatic are the eight surviving menhirs (standing stones), including a possible statue menhir on Chapel Down, St Martin's [28]; the stone row sometimes exposed on Higher Town Beach, St Martin's; and the four holed stones, one re-erected in Tresco Gardens [72]. The date and purpose of these is uncertain, but in Cornwall they are considered of late neolithic and early Bronze Age date. Menhirs are thought to have served as grave and memorial stones, territorial and

Old Man of Gugh menhir　　　　　©*Frank Gibson*

way markers, and stone rows may have had a processional use.

Visually least impressive, but most common amongst the ceremonial monuments is the simple cairn of which almost four hundred survive, the majority in large groups covering the main moorland tracts. These roughly circular mounds, constructed of small stones and earth, often surrounded by a kerb of boulders, are generally small and insignificant looking, being as little as 2.0 metres in diameter and 0.1 metres high. However, a number are very substantial (up to 22.0 metres across and 2.2 metres high) and some contain cists (boxes lined and capped with stone slabs), which also occur without a covering cairn and would have held a single cremation. The funerary purpose of most cairns is assumed rather than proven and some, at least, may be the result of field clearance, especially those lying within early fields or connected by boulder walls — for example on Shipman Head Down [13]. In Cornwall cairns date from 2000-1600 BC, but in Scilly, it seems likely that they overlapped with entrance graves in the middle Bronze Age and continued to be built during the Iron Age.

Long-lived traditions are also reflected in the material culture of early Scillonians. Similar pottery was used throughout the Bronze Age; using locally available clays, crude, coil-built, often poorly fired pots of a coarse granitic fabric were made. Jars, cooking pots, large storage vessels, cups and bowls were mainly left plain, but some had a collar of decoration. Combs were used to produce horizontal grooves and stamped decoration, lines of impressed circles were created by the end of a hollow stick or bone, and twisted cord impressions and applied lugs (decorative handles) were also common. A woven mat impression found on some bases is either a deliberate pattern or made by a mat or basket used to support the pot before firing. Traditions of working flint from locally collected beach pebbles also remained the same throughout the Bronze Age, when flint tools were essential to everyday life. By far the most numerous were scrapers for working animal hides, removing fish scales and working materials such as wood and antler. Awls, for piercing and boring were the second most common tool, perhaps reflecting a continued heavy reliance on leather rather than cloth (also suggested by the virtual absence of spindle whorls). Other flint tools were knives, choppers, arrowheads, strike-a-lights and burins (chisel-like tools for working bone and antler). Other types of stone were used to make quartz and granite hammer stones, quartz choppers, granite saddle and bowl querns for grinding grain into flour and

Possible statue menhir on Chapel Down, St Martin's

Stone Row on Higher Town Beach, St Martin's

pulverising foodstuffs (such as pulses), granite bowls for water storage, and greisen or soft granite oil lamps. Animal and bird bones were worked to produce awls, points, punches and gouges, and antlers were made into picks.

The term *Bronze Age* implies the introduction of metalworking; first of gold, then copper, followed by the alloying of tin with copper to produce bronze. However, in Scilly as in Cornwall the term represents a rather false chronological division. Only a dozen metal objects have been recorded and of these only four are from settlements (a bronze awl from May's Hill, St Martin's, and three unidentifiable bronze objects from Nornour [18]). The

remaining bronzes (a socketed axe, dagger, awl, earring, bracelet and two heavy torcs or necklets) are either unprovenanced, or from burials. An Irish gold bracelet dating to 1000 BC found on a beach on St Martin's probably originated from a hoard. Gold would always have been a rare metal used only for objects of prestige and display, but in Cornwall bronze was also not used for everyday tools until about 1400 BC. In Scilly, where new ideas were slow to catch on and where the lack of raw materials would have restricted local metal production, traditional tools of stone and bone stayed in use even longer, and may always have been most common.

Excavated cist on North Hill, Samson, from an engraving by John Blight, 1862

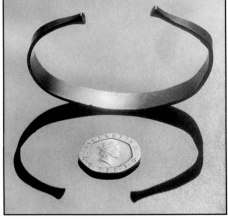

Late Bronze Age gold bracelet from St Martin's
© *Frank Gibson*

THE CONVENTIONAL division between the Bronze and Iron Age in British prehistory has become rather artificial. The change is now thought to have been less abrupt, the result of contact and exchange (and perhaps small-scale migration) rather than invasion from the continent, and, though iron gradually replaced bronze as the main metal for making tools and weapons, this did not coincide with other major social or cultural changes. In Cornwall these occurred both before and after 700BC, with a radical shift in pottery styles during the Late Bronze Age and widespread construction of hillforts and defended farmsteads from the 5th century BC. In Scilly we can assume an even later date for the development of iron working and though acid soils mean that iron preservation is poor, of the handful of early objects that have been found none can be dated any earlier than the late Iron Age and quite possibly were not made until the Romano-British period.

The overall picture is one of continuity of earlier traditions throughout most of the 1st millennium BC but with some changes occurring after 500BC. People still lived in circular houses (and in some cases the same houses themselves), farmed small rectilinear fields, used mainly stone tools and the same type of pottery. This was better made but remained essentially unchanged throughout the early Iron Age and continued for a while alongside new wares that appeared from the 5th century BC.

Known as **South West Decorated** or **Glastonbury** wares, these were also of granitic fabric and often still handmade, but were distinguishable from the earlier pottery, consisting of bowls and jars with burnished exteriors and incised and stamped decoration. They reflect greater contact with the mainland and from the 1st century BC pots were made from gabbroic clay from the Lizard peninsula (Cornwall) and cordons were used as a form of decoration on large vessels.

At roughly the same time as these changes in pottery Scilly's earliest fortifications were being constructed. The **cliff castle** was a coastal variation of the hill fort, consisting of stone or earth ramparts across the neck of a natural promontory providing protection from landward attack. In Cornwall they are thought to have served as economic and social centres under the control of tribal chiefs, presiding over and receiving tribute from surrounding farms. Only two definite cliff castles can be identified in Scilly (one on Shipman Head, Bryher [12], and another on the south-east side of St Mary's [39]), with a third possible example on Burnt Hill, St Martin's [27]. These three lie roughly equidistant from each other, on the edge of what would then have been one large island. It is tempting to suggest that they reflect the tribal divisions which existed in Scillonian society at this time.

At the end of the Iron Age cremation was replaced by inhumation in cist grave ceme-

Giant's Castle cliff castle, St Mary's

teries similar to those of the Cornish mainland. These graves were orientated north-south, and set roughly equidistant in lines, suggesting markers (perhaps of wood). They consist of oval or rectangular pits, lined with slabs set on edge or coursed walling and covered by capstones. Bodies were laid on their sides in crouched positions and often accompanied by grave goods: bronze (and occasionally iron) brooches (for fastening clothing or a shroud), pottery, amber or glass beads. The largest concentration of this type of grave was discovered in Hugh Town, on the west side of Porth Cressa. Excavations exposed fifteen cists, forming a single cemetery. These burials were Romano-British rather than Iron Age and, in Scilly, this may be true of this type in general. In the absence of any other distinctively Iron

Age funerary monuments, it is possible that the earlier tradition of burial beneath stone cairns continued throughout this period. A cairn piled over one of the cists at Porth Cressa reflects the earlier rite.

Placename evidence hints at the islands being a cult centre during the late Iron Age (water being one focus of religious practice at this time). Scilly is first mentioned as *insula sillina* by classical Roman writers of the 1st-3rd centuries AD, but the name is of native pre-Roman origin and may incorporate that of a Celtic female deity, similar if not identical to the water goddess, Sulis, worshipped at the hot springs of Bath. A carved stone on Chapel Down, St Martin's [28] may be the head and shoulders of a Celtic idol (possibly a crude depiction of the common horned god).

On the Fringe
AD43–410 ROMANO-BRITISH PERIOD

SILLINA OCCUPIED a very peripheral position in the Roman Empire, so remote that two heretic Spanish bishops were exiled there in AD 384. There is no evidence to suggest that the Islands were ever under direct rule or even formally conquered. Scilly may have been administered for Rome by its native leader(s), but even this seems improbable as, unlike Cornwall, Scilly was not a source of tin and its people were probably left largely to their own devices.

Simple stone houses were still the norm, but walls were now sometimes clay-mortared and rendered, and an excavated structure at Halangy Down, St Mary's [40], has much in common with the courtyard houses characteristic of West Cornwall during this period. A long narrow entrance passage leads through a massive enclosing wall into a sub-rectangular courtyard, off which are two good-sized oval and circular living rooms (one with a pentagonal recess in its wall—perhaps a sleeping compartment) and a tiny sub-circular chamber (maybe a store). This is the building's final form, the culmination of several progressive stages of construction from the late Iron Age to

the 2nd century AD. The Cornish examples had open courtyards but that at Halangy Down is thought to have been entirely roofed.

A mixed economy was still practised, but there were a few new developments. The pig was now completely domesticated and fowl were also kept. Red deer may have died out during the 2nd or 3rd centuries AD, but dogs and rabbits are recorded for the first time during this period. A few additional species of fish have also been identified; mullet, common eel, whiting and john dory. Birds of fresh or brackish water are more common; teal, long-tailed duck, scaup, common snipe, white stork, heron and possibly moorhen, swan and bittern. This may indicate a rising sea level creating pools behind dunes breached during severe storms, or merely dietary preferences.

Crouched inhumation cist burials continued throughout the Roman period. In contrast to earlier burial monuments, these cemeteries were situated adjacent to the houses of the living.

There appears to have been little direct Roman influence on the everyday tools and equipment used by Scillonians, but change did

The courtyard house at Halangy Down

come about as a result of the greater opportunity provided for contact and trade with the outside world. Only a few scraps of Samian ware (fine Roman tableware) have been found. Pots were made mainly from gabbroic clay of the Lizard peninsula, though local granitic wares also continued to be produced. Pottery was imported from Dorset, South Devon and Oxford, and to a lesser extent from Normandy and Brittany. Flint and bone tools were still important, but iron and bronze was also used: knives, arrowheads,

points and nails. Rotary querns (hand mills) were gradually replacing the earlier saddle and bowl types, making the grinding of corn more efficient.

Contrasting sharply with the general picture of Scilly as an essentially un-romanised rural community is the classical altar now in Tresco Abbey Gardens [72] and the shrine on Nornour [18]. Found last century in a well (perhaps a votive shaft) at the bottom of Garrison Hill, St Mary's, the altar may have originally stood in a Romano-Celtic cult building or temple on Mount Holles, below the Garrison walls, now covered by modern housing. It is uninscribed, but has side panels bearing reliefs of a long shafted axe and a cleaver, suggesting rites of a sacrificial nature. The collection of Roman objects from Nornour is astonishing and suggests that for as long as three hundred years (AD 70-380) this site was perhaps a shrine to a native marine goddess, attracting votive offer-

Front and side panels of the Roman altar found on St Mary's

Drawing: Rosemary Robertson

ings from travellers between Gaul and north and west Britain. A few Roman coins have been discovered elsewhere in Scilly, but the context and quantities in which these were found suggests none were used as currency.

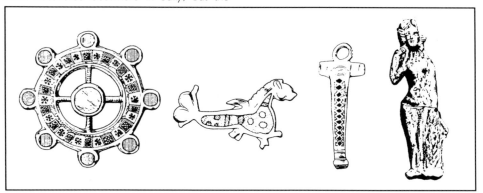

Bronze brooches and clay figurine from Nornour

after Dudley, 1968

From Cult to Christianity
AD410–1066 EARLY MEDIEVAL PERIOD

THE WITHDRAWAL of the Roman legions from Britain can have had little impact on the daily lives of people who had barely been affected by the occupation itself. Scilly also appears to have been unaffected by sporadic Anglo-Saxon conquests in East Cornwall. The story that Athelstan (King of Mercia AD 935-939) made a short visit to the Islands to deal with Scandinavian raiders is probably legend. The same applies to any connection with the mythical British king, Arthur, or Olaf Triggvason, a Viking supposedly converted to Christianity in Scilly in AD 994.

Where settlements have been excavated there is evidence for the continued occupation of stone houses built during the Romano-British period (and earlier). However, a few of Early Medieval date have been identified and these are now rectangular, allowing for a ridge roof and an interior free of supporting posts.

Early Medieval occupation is distinguished mainly by the presence of new types of pottery. Grass marked vessels (vertically-sided, flat-bottomed cooking pots and platters with chopped grass impressions on the underside of their bases) were handmade locally or in Cornwall, where the tradition probably began in the 7th century. From AD 900 bar-lugs (strap handles) were added to the inside rim of some cooking pots to allow suspension over a fire without the grass-rope or leather-strap hangings being burnt. As well as this local pottery, imported wheelmade wares arrived in Scilly as a result of long distance trade to West Britain and Ireland from the Mediterranean and France. The Islands benefitted from being a convenient point for sailors to land for fresh water and provisions, exchanged for East Mediterranean amphorae containing wine and olive oil, and barrels of Gaulish wine, accompanied by domestic pottery (jars, beakers, bowls and pitchers). A settlement on Tean [63] may have served as a small trading port for the rest of Scilly.

An important result of these external contacts was the introduction of Christianity during the late 5th or early 6th century. This may have been introduced from Cornwall, France or the Mediterranean. The earliest evidence is a 6th century tombstone [72] now incorporated into the later priory church on Tresco. Originally an upright pillar, it has a Latin inscription incorporating Celtic personal names and may have been associated with a nearby Early Christian cist cemetery, one of five identified in Scilly. Though these cemeteries are superficially similar to Romano-British ones, their graves are longer, narrower and coffin-shaped, aligned roughly east-west and contain extended skeletons facing east. They are occasionally covered by simple kerbed cairns or marked by small stones, like the sub-circular slab with a simple incised cross found in one cemetery.

Associated with the graves of the dead are the places where the living worshipped — tiny rectangular stone chapels aligned east-west with a doorway in their south side. Three survive in various states of ruin on St Helen's [24], Tean [63] and St Martin's [28], and others may once have stood on St Mary's, Samson, St Agnes and Tresco, where Early Christian cemeteries have been recorded. Only the St Helen's chapel has visible internal features: an altar block (with a small recess for housing holy relics) standing on a raised step at the east end and stone bench foundations along the other walls. Dating from the early 8th century AD, these early religious foundations have previously been interpreted as hermitages. This interpretation still holds good for St Helen's, but men, women and children were buried in the cemetery on Tean. The current model for sea level change suggests that most of the

St Helen's Chapel

present islands were still one land mass at this time. The chapels probably served mainly as Christian foci for the lay population of Scilly, similar to the parish churches of the later medieval period. However, the St Martin's example, because of its exposed position and apparent lack of associated cemetery, was perhaps a lighthouse chapel where a fire-beacon was maintained.

Christianity was now firmly established in Scilly but it would have assimilated some old pagan beliefs. For example, St Warna's holy well on St Agnes [5] is probably an early medieval structure, but the tradition of attributing supernatural powers to water originated in pre-Christian times.

Under English Rule
1066–1540 MEDIEVAL PERIOD

SHORTLY AFTER after the Norman Conquest the Islands became the property of the Crown of England, and from 1141, part of the Earldom then, after 1337, the Duchy of Cornwall. From the 12th century the administration of Scilly was split; Tavistock Abbey presided over the northern part, and the de Wika family of Week St Mary in north Cornwall (and later the Blanchminsters, also of north Cornwall) were proprietors of what are now St Mary's and St Agnes. Tavistock Abbey's interest had dwindled by the Reformation and in 1547, the whole of Scilly was acquired by Thomas

Seymour (the Lord Admiral).

The centre of the ecclesiastical administration was St Nicholas' Priory; its ruined church still visible in the Gardens on Tresco [72]. This island, together with Bryher, formed a larger land mass, known first as **Rentemen** (meaning unknown) and later as **Saint Nicholas' Ile**, and may have been more important than St Mary's during this period. The priory is first alluded to in a charter of 1120 granting Tavistock Abbey all the churches of Scilly (with their appurtenances and land), but it is assumed to have been well established by this date. Pirates and raiders

preying on English mer-
chantmen may have
been part of the reason
behind Henry I's grant,
and the monk, Turold,
sent to take charge was
instructed to 'keep a
firm peace'. As prior,
he would have been
one of only two or
three brethren, with
servants (Scillonian or
from Tavistock) living
nearby and farming the
adjoining land. Evidence
for the monks being
involved in long dis-
tance trade is provided
by a reference in the
Orkneyinga-saga (the
ancient history of Ork-
ney compiled around
1200) to the plundering
of one of their mer-

St Nicholas' Priory church, Tresco

chant ships. Split dried fish and seabirds from
the Islands may have been exchanged for
Cornish pottery, tin, slate and cloth; Breton
salt, linen and canvas; Irish cloaks and wood;
French wine and pottery; and Spanish wine
and fruit. Pottery was also imported from
other parts of southern England; Dorset,
Wiltshire, Bristol and Exeter. The priory may
have collected tolls for anchorage in St Helen's
Pool, probably the chief harbour in medieval
times.

From the 11th century there appears to have
been a general revival in Christianity in Scilly,
which increased under Tavistock's influence;
existing establishments were improved and
new ones built, for example, on St Helen's
[24], and at Old Town, St Mary's [46]. By 1461,
St Helen's church was in a state of disrepair
and, like St Nicholas' Priory (hardly mentioned
in documentary sources after the 15th century),
it may have become ruined before the
Reformation. The priory does not even feature
in a list of Tavistock's possessions drawn up at
that time.

Secular rule was based at Old Town, known in
the 12th century as *Ennor*. A Cornish name
meaning simply 'the land' and originally

referring to most of Scilly, it had by this time
been reduced in scope to refer primarily to St
Mary's and secondarily to its main settlement.
The monks of Tavistock Abbey had an
alternative name for it; *La Val*, Norman French
for 'Down-there' or 'At-the-bottom', referring
to its low-lying situation. A major reason for
the choice of this site was its natural harbour,
Porthenor, whose medieval quay still survives
[48]. Though the initial focus was the church,
this shifted from 1244 with the erection of a
castle [38] on top of a rock outcrop
overlooking the Porth's eastern side. In the
early 14th century it was held by Ranulph de
Blanchminster in return for maintaining 12
men-at-arms for keeping the peace. As
tenant-in-chief he paid a yearly tribute to the
king of three hundred puffins or 6s 8d. (Puffins,
considered fish rather than fowl, could be
eaten during Lent, and their feathers were also
valuable, but money seems always to have
been paid). This arrangement was not untrou-
bled. In 1308 the king's coroner, William Le
Poer, was imprisoned at *La Val* for carrying
away a whale cast up on Ranulph's land, and
only released after he had paid a fine of 100s.
In 1345 Ranulph was unable to raise his full

Old Town — site of Scilly's main medieval settlement; Castle Ennor is the wooded knoll in the top left corner, the medieval quay lies bottom right

rent because 600 Welsh sailors on an expedition to Brittany driven into Scilly and becalmed for twenty days, stripped the Islands bare (taking corn, animals, bread and other goods) and generally caused havoc.

This incident illustrates Scilly's vulnerability. Strategically placed, but poorly defended, it was easy prey for 12th century Viking raiders and pirates who were probably the reason for the decline of the religious establishments on Tresco and St Helen's.

Though Old Town was the main settlement in the Islands, the location of others is revealed by documentary and placename evidence and medieval pottery scatters; Churchtown and Lower Town on St Martin's, Old Grimsby and Borough Farm on Tresco, Norrard and Southard on Bryher, and Middle Town on St Agnes. Others lie undetected beneath farms and hamlets still occupied today, and modern housing in Hugh Town covers a hillock (Mount Holles) on which a medieval keep may have stood.

Block House, south of Old Grimsby

Forts, Famine and Fortune
1540–1945 POST MEDIEVAL AND MODERN

IN 1549, ONLY two years after acquiring Scilly, Lord Admiral Seymour was accused of plotting against the King (Edward VI) and using the Islands as a base for piracy. His execution marked the beginning of the Godolphin connection with Scilly. The heads of this Cornish family were initially appointed as Captains of the Isles, but in 1570 Elizabeth I granted Francis Godolphin a thirty-eight year lease in return for an annual rent of £20. After two hundred and eight-two years of almost continuous rule, the link was severed when Scilly returned to the direct control of the Duchy in 1831. Three years later, Augustus Smith, a member of an old Hertfordshire family, became Lord Proprietor. His descendants still lease Tresco from the Duchy, which continues to own most of Scilly.

From the mid-16th century English foreign policy exerted much greater influence on Scilly. War with France led to the construction of many new defences around the coast of Southern England, and in Scilly, strategically important at the entrance to the Western Approaches, resulted in the building of fortifications to guard the main approaches, harbours and anchorages. Erected between 1548 and 1554, they include King Charles' Castle [68] and three blockhouses; one on the site of Cromwell's Castle [69], another south of Old Grimsby [67] (both on Tresco) and a third on the north-east coast of St Mary's. A fort —Harry's Walls [41]—was begun but never completed on Mount Flagon, overlooking St Mary's Pool, and guns were mounted on The Hugh (perhaps in an earlier castle on Mount Holles or in a fort on the south side known as *The Folly*). Henry VIII maintained a garrison at Ennor Castle, from 1544-47 and during Edward VI's reign it continued to defend Old Town harbour, being used as the armoury for the main body of the garrison which by 1554 consisted of 150 men.

During Elizabeth I's reign (1558-1603) the defences were run down, with, surprisingly, no special provision being made against the Spanish Armada of 1588. However, the threat of a second invasion fleet led, in 1593, to the building of Star Castle [54] on The Hugh. Work was supervised by Robert Adams, England's leading expert on coastal defences, and shortly after its completion a curtain wall (with bastions, gateway and sallyports) was constructed across the neck of the headland [54] with an extra-mural battery on Mount Holles. A magazine and other buildings were erected within the defences and a quay [42] built in the harbour below. From this time The Hugh (originally pronounced *Hoo* and meaning 'elevated ground' or 'promontory') became the main focus of military activity.

During the Civil War (1642-46), Scilly was caught up in the drama of national events when the Islands became a Royalist stronghold.

Star Castle from a 1720 engraving by John Seago

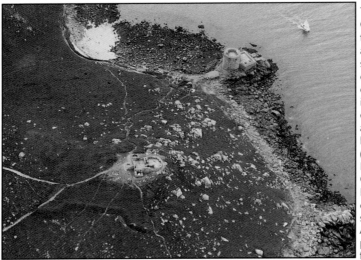

King Charles' Castle with its Civil War earthwork and Cromwell's Castle

Gun and semaphore tower on Telegraph Hill

The garrison at Star Castle was strengthened and batteries and breastwork constructed around the coast of St Mary's and on most of the other islands. Documentary evidence also exists for an inland fortification or barracks on St Mary's (known as **New Fort**). In March 1646, Prince Charles (later Charles II) and most of his council sailed to Scilly, staying there until mid-April when they slipped past a Parliamentary fleet to the safety of Jersey. Following the fall of Pendennis Castle, the last Royalist stronghold on the mainland, Scilly surrendered on September 12th. The next year Parliament appointed Colonel Buller as governor (Francis Godolphin being under close surveillance in Cornwall), but in September 1648, while he was attending church, his soldiers revolted. With the Islands once again under Royalist command, Sir John Grenville became governor, but under him privateering led to piracy, passing ships being plundered regardless of nationality. In 1651 the Dutch under Admiral van Tromp sailed to capture Scilly, arriving at the same time as a Parliamentary fleet led by Admiral Blake. The Dutch backed off and Blake, after being deliberately led astray by a local pilot, captured Tresco and, when negotiations for surrender broke down, pounded The Hugh with fire from his ships and Oliver's Battery [71]. The Royalists finally surrendered on 23rd May 1651 and sailed off ten days later. With the security of the Islands still threatened by the Dutch fleets, Cromwell's Castle [69] was erected to replace King Charles' in the defence of New Grimsby Harbour.

The Restoration of the Monarchy in 1660 saw the return of the Godolphin family as governors. Fifty years later the War of the Spanish Succession prompted England to strengthen its defences against France and Spain. In Scilly this meant a thirty-year programme supervised by

St Martin's signal station and daymark

Tresco World War I seaplane base, with concrete standing, ramp and rails surviving

Master Gunner Abraham Tovey, during which the curtain wall on The Hugh was rebuilt and extended around most of the headland, which became known as The Garrison [**54**]. Many of the older buildings surviving on The Garrison and in Hugh Town were erected at this time and the quay was also rebuilt.

Little more was done until the Napoleonic Wars (1794-1815) led to the construction of two circular guntowers on St Mary's (on The Garrison [**54**] and Telegraph Hill [**53**]), a signal station on St Martin's [**28**] and various lookouts and watch houses.

In 1863 The Garrison defences were disbanded. An unsuccessful scheme to make Scilly a naval base resulted in the building of several large batteries between 1896 and 1905 — two on The Garrison [**54**] and one at Bant's Carn. All guns were removed by 1906.

During both World Wars The Garrison accommodated up to a thousand servicemen. In World War I a naval and seaplane base was established, first at Porth Mellon on St Mary's, but then rebuilt south of New Grimsby on Tresco. The concrete standings for both survive and on Tresco the ramp and iron rails for trundling the planes down to the water. With the fall of France at the beginning of World War II, Scilly was heavily fortified, suffered frequent strafing and occasional bombing by enemy aircraft, and became a centre of activity against German submarines. Machine-gun posts were built around the coast of St Mary's, where Hurricane fighter planes and air-sea rescue launches were also stationed.

Everyday life in Scilly was never easy and could be very harsh. After the Napoleonic Wars distress was so widespread that a relief committee was set up on the mainland and

Mount Todden watch house

1900 battery (Woolpack) on top of the Garrison

A kelp pit

£9,000 raised. It was not until Augustus Smith took over the lease of the Islands in 1834 that economic stability was established.

Farming continued to be the mainstay of the economy; pigs and cattle were raised and potatoes and wheat were the main crops. Grain was ground at communal windmills, on The Garrison (1690s-1726) [54], Peninnis Head (1726-1834) [50] and Buzza Hill (1834-late 19th century) [36]. During the 19th century earlier and better varieties of potato were introduced, the surplus being exported to the Mediterranean.

Fishing was an important source of food but never a major industry. However, ling caught on long-lines and dried, salted and exported was apparently famous; a letter of 1803 from Lord Nelson in Toulon to a friend in Plymouth thanks him for his present of Scilly Ling. Most of the relief money raised for the Islands in 1819 was used to start a mackerel and pilchard fishery. Fish cellars were built on Tresco and boats and nets provided, but the venture was unsuccessful.

There was little tin to mine. The only recorded remains are a line of pits and open-works of an abortive 17th century venture on Castle Down, Tresco [68].

In 1684 the kelp industry was introduced to Scilly from Falmouth, by the Nance family who settled on Tean for several generations. For one hundred and fifty years it was one of the main forms of employment. Seaweed (kelp) was collected, dried and burnt in small stone-lined pits located close to the waters edge. This foul-smelling process produced soda ash, which was shipped to Bristol and Gloucester to be used in the manufacture of glass, soap and bleach. After the Napoleonic Wars, increased foreign supplies of soda ash and new chemical processes for the manufacture of alkali led to the decline of the Scilly's industry, which ceased in 1835. Though a hundred fires are said to have once burnt, the

Gigshed at Great Porth, Bryher

remains of only a dozen kelp pits are now visible.

Smuggling was an essential part of the economy during the 18th century, but was made more difficult by the stationing of a protection vessel in the Islands after 1784. An Act of Parliament in 1790 allowed the cost of court proceedings to be met out of the sale of seizures, and an added inducement was given to revenue officers by allowing them to keep a small share of the proceeds. After this smuggling declined, but some of the caches where contraband was hidden can still be seen, for example the subterranean stone-lined chamber in the garden of **Smugglers** on the east side of Tresco.

Between 1720 and 1870 Scilly (especially St Agnes and St Martin's) was home to many pilots, who ensured that ships had a safe passage through the Islands and beyond. By the beginning of the 19th century piloting was restricted to fewer individuals, but in 1850 there were still fifteen good pilot boats—cutters and **gigs**. When not in use the gigs were housed in narrow sheds, like those poking out from beneath the dune at Lower Town, St Martin's.

right: St Agnes Lighthouse from a 1720 engraving by John Seago

below: Round Island Lighthouse at the turn of the century   © *Frank Gibson*

The LIGHT HOUSE In St Agne's Illand.

Shipbuilding began in Scilly in the 18th century, and became an important industry during the 1830s. Though Augustus Smith helped to organise and finance this development, the companies were set up by Islanders purchasing £5 and £10 shares. The industry flourished and by the mid-19th century there were five ship-building yards on St Mary's and fifty-nine registered ships. These wooden sailing vessels were crewed and skippered by Scillonians, the cargoes and the ships being the property of the shareholders. They traded all over the world, but mainly conveyed potatoes (and other goods) from Ireland to the Mediterranean. Eventually, unable to compete with steam-powered iron ships, Scilly's industry came to an end.

The importance of the sea in terms of employment, trade and communications is reflected in the archaeological record. As well as kelp pits, gigsheds and smugglers' caches, there are ruined quays and slipways, a 17th century day mark (on St Martin's [28]), several lighthouses and an 18th century isolation hospital. Known as the Pest House, this was built on St Helen's [26] after a 1754 Act of Parliament decreed that any plague-ridden ship north of Cape Finisterre heading for England should anchor off this island. Trinity House's involvement in Scilly began as early as 1680 when they built their first lighthouse on St Agnes [1], superseded in 1911 by one on Peninnis head. The Bishop Rock Lighthouse [73] was built last century first in iron and later in granite, the remains of an associated blacksmith's shop and workers quarters surviving on the nearby rocky island of Rosevear [74]. Round Island Lighthouse was erected in 1887, around the same time as Bishop Rock was being strengthened.

At the time when shipbuilding had come to an end and the early potato harvests were failing, Scilly's flower industry began. It started in a small way around 1879, when William Trevellick of Rocky Hill Farm, St Mary's sent an experimental consignment of cut flowers to Covent Garden in a hat box. Its long term success was largely due to Augustus Smith's nephew, T A Dorrien-Smith, who studied the Dutch system of cultivation and introduced new kinds of bulbs. The remains of steam-heated glasshouses and packing sheds can be seen on many farms. The through railway connection from Penzance established in 1859 and its link with a steamer service begun the previous year, made the transportation of flowers to market viable. It also marked the beginning of the tourist industry which now forms the largest part of Scilly's economy.

In 1551 the population was around two hundred and fifty, but gradually rose to become almost ten times this figure today. After 1570 Francis Godolphin induced Cornish people to settle in Scilly, notably on

The Pest House, St Helen's

St Martin's. However, this island was largely deserted during the Civil War, when many tenements became ruined or laid waste by soldiers, only two surviving to be recorded in the 1652 Parliamentary survey of the Islands. On St Mary's, Tresco, Bryher and probably St Agnes, occupation continued unbroken throughout the post-medieval period; not so on St Helen's where after the abandonment of the religious establishment by at least the mid-16th century, re-occupation did not occur until the building of the isolation hospital in 1764. By the time of the 1652 survey Tean and Samson were also uninhabited. Tean was resettled by the Nance family from 1684 until after 1800 when they moved to St Martin's. The resettlement of Samson probably took place around 1683 when new holdings were being established on St Martin's. By 1834, when Augustus Smith took over the lease of Scilly, a vulnerably small population, chronic water shortage and fragmented farms made life on Samson very difficult. As part of his economic reform Smith initially encouraged people to leave and in 1855 evicted those few who remained. Their ruined houses and stone-walled fields lend a sad air to South Hill, which Smith later enclosed in an abortive attempt to create a deer park [**60**].

For Augustus Smith, an energetic Victorian interested in 'improving the lot of the labouring classes', Scilly (for years misruled by the agents of absentee landlords and struggling under difficult economic conditions) represented the ideal challenge. Adopting an autocratic role, he began by reallocating farm lands, which had become minute and scattered by sub-division, and introduced a system of inheritance by which land passed only to the eldest son, all other offspring being forced to find alternative employment. Smith encouraged this by financing existing and new local industries, building schools on all the main islands and making education compulsory (thirty years before this became law on the mainland). He broke with tradition by becoming a resident landlord and erecting his house not on St Mary's but on Tresco, next to the remains of the medieval priory, around which he created a sub-tropical garden out of bare moorland. In fulfilment of a condition of his lease, in 1838 Smith built a new quay (connecting Hugh Town Old Quay with Rat Island) and St Mary's church.

Scilly's other churches were either modified or rebuilt during the 19th century, though all have earlier origins. Each has its own individual character; St Martin's [**30**] and Old Town's church [**46**] are described in the gazetteer, Tresco's (1879) copies the cruciform pattern of the priory church, Bryher's (1742) has a sturdy west tower and the church on St Agnes (1821) is an unpretentious building with a fine stained glass window. John Wesley visited Scilly in 1743 and Methodist chapels were later built throughout the Islands. Of particular interest is the dissenting chapel of 1845 at Higher Town, St Martin's and the Georgian chapel in Garrison Lane, Hugh Town (now a store, with some of its internal fittings re-used in the late 19th century Methodist Church) The Roman Catholic Chapel, **Stella Maris**, was originally built as St Mary's Girls School (1860).

Ruines of the Abby on Trescaw

GAZETTEER

This gazetteer contains a representative sample of sites from all periods, most very accessible, but some on uninhabited islands or partially overgrown. It is designed to be used in conjunction with the Ordnance Survey Outdoor Leisure (1:25000) map, on which many sites are marked. National Grid references are given (eg **SV 908123**) with the name on the map, if any, (eg *Standing stone*). Sites are arranged alphabetically (ignoring any St. prefix) by Island and numbered on an outline map of Scilly, to be found on the centre pages.

The Isles of Scilly Museum on St Mary's has an interesting display of artefacts from excavated sites and some finds from Scilly can also be seen in Royal Cornwall Museum, Truro.

IMPORTANT
Some sites have undergone conservation work and visitors are asked to abide by notices requesting that they use redirected paths or avoid repaired areas. Please report any damage immediately to Cornwall Archaeological Unit (Tel: 01872 323603) and the Isles of Scilly Environmental Trust (Tel: 01720 422153). Please deposit any archaeological artefacts found at the Isles of Scilly Museum and report the find to the Archaeological Unit.

KEY TO LOCAL SITE MAPS

- ● Cairn
- ◎ Entrance grave
- ○ Round house
- ⋀ Prehistoric field system
- ▬ Bank and ditch
- ‐ ‐ ‐ Footpaths

ST AGNES

1 ST AGNES LIGHTHOUSE
SV 880082 *Lighthouse (dis)*
The very first lighthouse erected by Trinity House, in 1680. The tower's three-stage construction is still evident, though the lantern has been changed. Light was originally supplied by a coal fire and the last iron brazier used is now in Tresco Abbey Gardens [**72**]. In 1790

1: St Agnes Lighthouse earlier this century

©*Frank Gibson*

4: An early photograph of Troy Town Maze
© *Frank Gibson*

that was replaced by an oil lamp. The lighthouse was superseded in 1911 by a steel one on Peninnis Head, St Mary's, but still serves as a prominent daymark. Members of the public can only view the lighthouse from outside its walled garden.

2 CASTELLA DOWNS FIELD SYSTEM
SV 875078 *marked but not named*
The fragmentary remains of a rectilinear prehistoric field system are visible on the downland north and south of Troy Town maze [**4**]. Five lengths of boulder wall, incorporating large orthostats and rock outcrops, run across the slope down towards the cliff edge.

3 PORTH ASKIN GIGSHED
SV 882074
Opening onto the low clifftop on the northeast side of Porth Askin is a rectangular ruin which once housed a pilot gig. Now largely concealed by blown sand. It appears on the 1889 map as one of three sheds here.

4 TROY TOWN MAZE
SV 875078 Maze
Close to the cliff edge on the west side of Castella Down is a circular maze of rounded beach stones forming a labyrinth pattern known as the Game of Troy. Traditionally it was laid out in 1729 by the bored son of the local lighthouse keeper, but an earlier origin is possible (the rebuilding of the maze in December 1988 will have destroyed any buried clues). Troy Town maze is unique in

Britain, resembling the stone mazes of Scandinavia. There are more recent copies elsewhere in Scilly.

5 ST WARNA'S WELL
SV 880078 *St Warna's Well*
A holy well dedicated to St Warna, allegedly capable of attracting shipwrecks and invoked by

5: St Warna's Well

offerings of crooked pins. Three stone steps lead down to a small underground chamber covered by a single capstone. Though possibly medieval (or earlier) this well has probably been restored since being described as 'little more than a hole' in 1890.

6 WINGLETANG DOWN CAIRN CEMETERY

SV 883075 *Cairns*

Forty-three cairns survive on this atmospheric stretch of moorland as low circular mounds, some retained by kerbs of granite boulders. Gorse obscures those in the centre of the down, but many can be seen on the surrounding heather-covered areas. Those on the north-east edge are connected by prehistoric field walls.

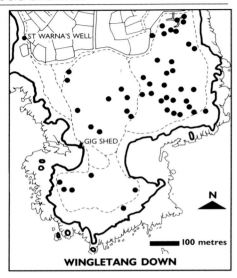

WINGLETANG DOWN

BRYHER

7 GREAT PORTH GIGSHEDS

SV 875147 *marked but not named*

Two disused gigsheds above the beach on the Porth's north-east side. The northern shed had its roof of thatched rushes in 1966, but is now very ruinous. The southern one stands to roof height, but has lost its red pantile roof.

12: The Rampart of Shipman Head Cliff Castle

8 GREEN BAY FIELD SYSTEM

SV 879146 *marked but not named*

Below high water are the remains of a prehistoric field system of boulder walls in an irregular pattern of sub-rectangular and square enclosures. The majority lie halfway along the beach, with outlying walls to the north-east and south.

9 GWEAL HILL ENTRANCE GRAVE AND CAIRNS

SV 87149 *Chambered Cairn, Cairns*

On the crest of this hill an entrance grave and two cairns survive in close proximity. The **entrance grave** lies on the east side of the group and has a north-south chamber of slabs set on edge and natural rock, set centrally within a low mound. No capstones survive. The **western cairn** is a prominent mound incorporating outcropping rock surrounded by a kerb of five stones. In its centre are the remains of a stone cist. The **central cairn** has a low irregular profile and no internal structure, but one possible kerbstone.

10 KITCHEN PORTH QUAY

SV 880155

Below high water in the middle of this Porth are substantial remains of an old quay consisting of a slightly curving stone platform, faced with large boulders.

II SAMSON HILL ENTRANCE GRAVES AND CAIRNS

SV 878142 *Cairns*

Two entrance graves and two cairns occupy the hilltop. At the eastern end lies an oval cairn, enclosing a rock outcrop and surrounded by a kerb of 21 stones. A few metres north-east is an overgrown **entrance grave**: a mound, revetted by 10 neatly-set kerbstones and other natural rocks. The central hollow is probably the remains of a chamber. At the west end of the hilltop, an irregular D-shaped kerbed **cairn** built against a natural rock also has remains of a chamber running along the outcrop. Two metres north-east on a

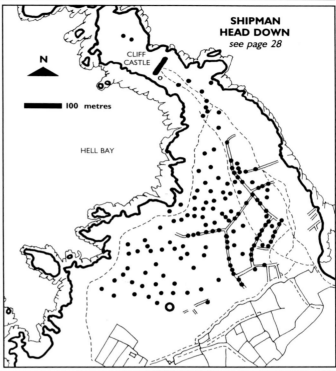

SHIPMAN HEAD DOWN
see page 28

CLIFF CASTLE

N

100 metres

HELL BAY

14: Watch Hill

THE ISLES OF SCILLY

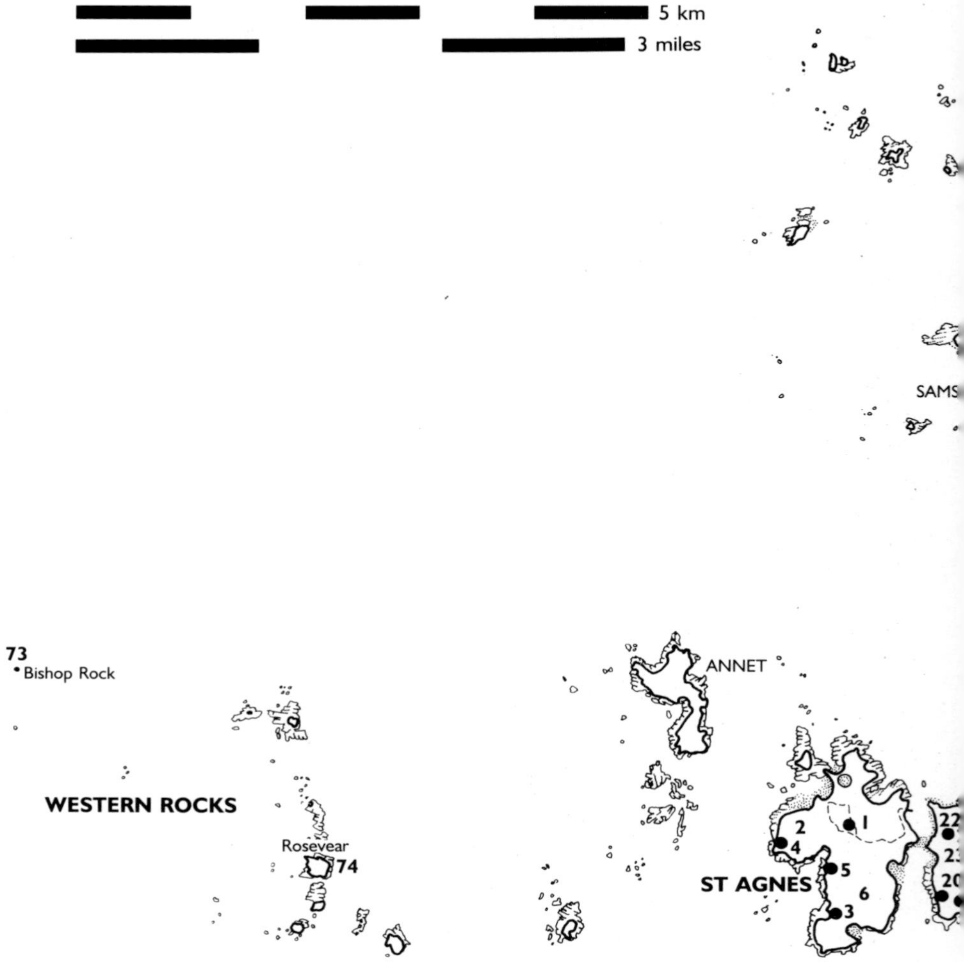

5 km
3 miles

SAMS

73
• Bishop Rock

ANNET

WESTERN ROCKS

Rosevear
74

ST AGNES

1
2
4
5
6
3

22
2
2
20

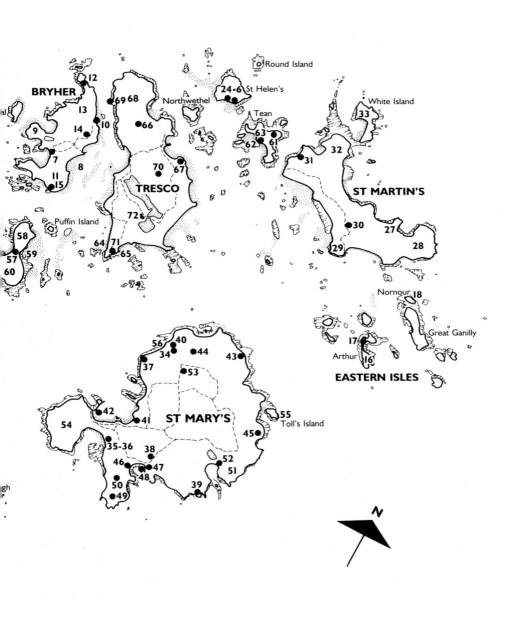

Round Island

BRYHER

12

69 68

Northwethel

24-6 St Helen's

13

White Island

33

Tean

10

14

66

63

9

62 61

32

31

St MARTIN'S

7

8

70 67

11

15

TRESCO

72

Puffin Island

27

30

58

64 71

29

28

57 59

65

60

Nornour 18

Great Ganilly

17

Arthur 16

EASTERN ISLES

56 40

34 44

43

37

53

42

54

41

ST MARY'S

55

Toll's Island

45

35-36

38

46 47

52

48

51

50

39

49

N

natural eminence of bare rock by the footpath is a simple **cairn** with a slight central disturbance.

12 SHIPMAN HEAD CLIFF CASTLE
SV 876161 *Fort*

The remains of an Iron Age cliff castle — a substantial rampart extending from a prominent rock outcrop to the cliff edge — cuts off this storm-battered headland from the rest of the Island. Surviving as a bank of tumbled boulders, with some facing stones, the rampart was originally revetted on both sides. On the cliff edge to the south-east, a curving bank may be the remains of a round house or cairn.

13 SHIPMAN HEAD DOWN *see page 25*
Entrance grave, cairns and field system
SV 876156 *Chambered Cairn, Cairns, Field System*

Cairns (134) are scattered over the Down. Most are small, circular stone and earth platforms, often built out from the natural slope and partially revetted by a stone kerb. A few are boulder cairns constructed around natural outcrops. Though assumed to have been used for burial, some may represent stone clearance, especially as many are linked by **prehistoric field walls**. These boulder alignments, with low stone and earth banks,

divide up the central and eastern parts of the Down in a rectilinear pattern. The field system has been heavily robbed and would originally have been more extensive. On its south-west edge is a very **large mutilated cairn** with a poorly defined hollow near its centre, traces of a kerb, and a possible capstone at its north-east end.

14 WATCH HILL
Watch house
SV 880052

Adjacent to the triangulation point is a small walled enclosure used as a lookout for shipping. Troutbeck (1796) records a watch house, which gave its name to the hill, and the structure standing today may be the original or a later one built on the same site.

15 WORKS CARN ENTRANCE GRAVE
SV 878141 *Chambered Cairn*

An oval-shaped cairn built out from the slope incorporating at least three natural rocks, is revetted by an almost complete kerb of large orthostats (21 visible) with a chamber extending for much of its length. The sides are of slabs set on edge, with some coursed walling. Five capstones remain, two still in place.

17: Southern entrance grave on Middle Arthur, Eastern Isles
see opposite

16 GREAT ARTHUR
Entrance graves, cairns, field system
SV 942135 *Cairns*

Three entrance graves and two cairns, connected by a prehistoric **boulder wall**, form a linear group along the ridge of Great Arthur. The best **entrance grave**, to the north-east, has a circular mound with a coursed stone revetment and a centrally placed chamber with three capstones. The other **two entrance graves** are ruinous, their chambers only evident as sub-rectangular depressions. A triangulation point has been built on top of one. The **two cairns** are of a type uncommon in Scilly, consisting of a low ring bank with stones protruding.

17 MIDDLE ARTHUR ENTRANCE GRAVES
SV 939138 *Chambered Cairn*

Two well-preserved entrance graves. The **northern grave** consists of a rectangular chamber in a partially kerbed mound, the chamber sides constructed of slabs and coursed stones, with four capstones slightly displaced. The **southern grave** is a platform cairn retained by nine kerbstones surrounding a boat-shaped chamber of orthostatic slabs, apparently closed at both ends like a cist, but the south end may be formed by a displaced capstone. Excavations in 1953 produced fragments of a large funerary urn, together with flint and bone.

18 NORNOUR SETTLEMENT AND SHRINE
SV 944147 *Settlement*

A complex of 11 excavated circular stone buildings just above high water (buildings 3 and 4 covered by beach stones). The buildings were continually modified during their occupation — from the 2nd millennium BC to the 4th century AD, though not all were in use simultaneously. Internal features included radial stone partitions, stone-lined hearths and pits, stone benches, bowls and querns. During the Bronze and Iron Ages the settlement was probably home for a single extended family. During the Roman period buildings 1 and 2 may have served as a shrine (the rest of the site being abandoned by this time). Votive offerings included 280 brooches, 84 Roman coins, 35 bronze rings, 11 bronze bracelets and bangles, 2 bronze spoons, 24 glass beads, numerous fragments of glass vessels, miniature pots and pieces of Gallic clay figurines (representations of a nursing mother and pseudo-Venus). There is a fine display of the finds from Nornour in the Isles of Scilly Museum.

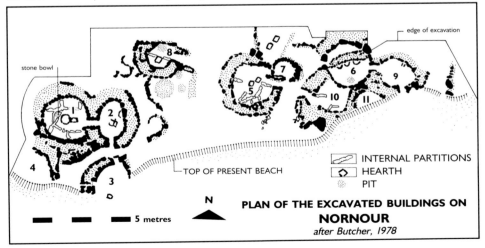

edge of excavation

stone bowl

INTERNAL PARTITIONS
HEARTH
PIT

TOP OF PRESENT BEACH

5 metres

N

PLAN OF THE EXCAVATED BUILDINGS ON
NORNOUR
after Butcher, 1978

GUGH

19 CARN OF WORKS
Battery and entrance grave
SV 891080

A Civil War **battery** shown on a 1792 map and called *The Works*. Consisting of a pentagonal rubble and earth platform, it abuts the outcrop known as Carn of Works and has distinct buttresses. Beyond the north-east and south-east faces are the footings of an outer line of defence, designed to provide a walkway between it and the main battery. A possible magazine in the platform's north-east corner re-uses the chamber of an **entrance grave** whose visible remains are an upright slab and capstone. The curve of the battery on this side may reflect the circular edge of the entrance grave.

Warning: during spring and early summer this part of Gugh is used by nesting colonies of black-backed gulls.

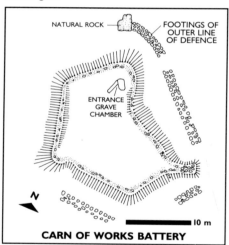

CARN OF WORKS BATTERY

20 CLAPPER OF WORKS ENTRANCE GRAVE AND CAIRNS
SV 890079

This **entrance grave** has a chamber extending almost its whole diameter. Four capstones remain. Nineteen simple **cairns** lie to the north and north-east.

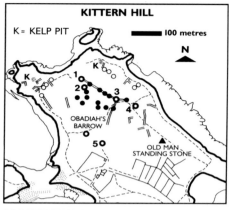

21 KITTERN HILL
Round houses, field system, cairns, entrance graves, kelp pit
SV 888087 *Cairns, Hut Circles*

Round houses survive on the north-east and north-west sides of Kittern Hill. Each comprises a small sub-circular terrace cut into the slope, edged on its downhill side by low turf-covered stone walls. Associated are the fragmentary remains of a **field system**; a rectilinear pattern of boulder walls connecting part of the cairn cemetery. Most of the 17 **cairns** are simple mounds, but three are **entrance graves** and three others may have housed chambers. A triangulation point cemented to the top of a prominent cairn (**1**) may obscure a ruined chamber or cist. South of this an impressive entrance grave (**2**) has a well-defined chamber with coursed walling and five capstones (one fallen). At the south-east end of the main field wall lies another entrance grave (**3**) with an earth-filled chamber but no capstones. South-east again another prominent mound (**4**) has two distinct depressions in its centre; perhaps the remains of a chamber. On the hill's south-west side lies Obadiah's Barrow [**22**] and at Carn Valla, another possible entrance grave (**5**) consisting of a cairn with several large stones which may be capstones. On the clifftop on the north and north-west side of Kittern Hill are two stone-lined **kelp pits**.

22 OBADIAH'S BARROW
Entrance grave
SV 888085 *Obadiah's Barrow*
This impressive entrance grave was excavated in 1901 by George Bonsor, and named after Obadiah Hicks with whom he lodged on St Agnes. Extending almost right across its kerbed cairn is a chamber with coursed walls, four of six capstones remaining, some are displaced. This is one of only four entrance graves in Scilly with a short passage leading to the chamber entrance. Also unusual is that the entrance is constricted by two projecting jamb stones, originally closed by a small rectangular slab. Bonsor found the chamber disturbed but largely intact. A deposit of blackish soil on the paved floor contained parts of a contracted male skeleton. Above were the remains of about a dozen urns (one virtually intact and now in the Isles of Scilly Museum) upside down over deposits of cremated bone. A fragment of a bronze awl and a hammer-stone were also found.

23 OLD MAN OF GUGH
Menhir
SV 890084 *Standing Stone*
This leaning menhir, 2.4 metres high, is a prominent feature on the skyline. George Bonsor dug around its base in 1900 but found nothing.

ST HELEN'S

24 ST ELIDIUS' HERMITAGE
Ecclesiastical complex
SV 901168 *Hermitage and church (remains of)*
The excavated stone remains of a multi-phased ecclesiastical complex. This site initially con-sisted of a small 8th century chapel and circular living cell associated with five graves, within a half-acre walled enclosure. The chapel has an altar's block (with a recess for housing holy relics) on a raised step, with bench foundations along the inside of other walls. This was a hermitage whose founder — perhaps St Eli-dius — may have lived in the circular cell and been buried in one of the graves. During the early 11th century a rectangular church was built. This was extended in the mid-12th century (by rebuilding the east end and adding a north aisle), when the circular cell was refurbished, three rectangular domestic rooms built and the precinct wall re-modelled. The 12th century church was in a state of disrepair by 1461 and was probably in ruins by the Reformation.

25 ST HELEN'S FIELD SYSTEM
SV 900170 *Field System*
The remains of a two-phased field system covering the southern half of the island. The earlier boundaries (boulder walls, stony banks and lynchets) are probably associated with St Elidius' Chapel [24], later drystone walls being contemporary with the Pest House [26]. The pattern of fields is predominantly rectilinear.

26 PEST HOUSE
Isolation hospital, quay
SV 899168 *Pest House*
A small unroofed building erected in 1764 as an **isolation hospital**. The hospital has single storey granite walls surviving to roof height and a brick chimney. It had a square main room and an annexe later subdivided. None of the rooms interconnect, but there is a blocked window between the two smaller ones. The base of a small porch survives in front of the main chamber door. Internal features include timber lintels, a small fireplace and traces of wall plaster. Associated with the Pest House is a sandy slip-way bordered on each side by a stone-built **quay** or breakwater.

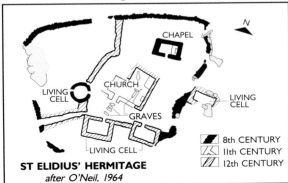

ST ELIDIUS' HERMITAGE
after O'Neil, 1964

8th CENTURY
11th CENTURY
12th CENTURY

27 BURNT HILL CLIFF CASTLE OR SETTLEMENT

SV 936160

Two prehistoric **round houses** and associated fieldwalls. Though perhaps an Iron Age cliff castle because of its promontory location, none of the walls appear substantial enough to have formed a line of defence and an unenclosed settlement is more likely. Each hut consists of a levelled area enclosed by a circle of boulders set on edge. The **field system** comprises boulder walls, slightly lynchetted, standing a maximum of 0.6 metres high.

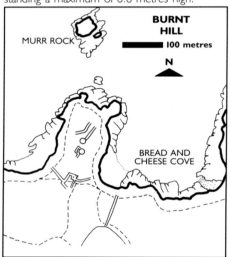

28 CHAPEL DOWN

Day Mark, chapel, signal station, field system, cairns, entrance grave, menhir and statue menhir/ Celtic idol

SV 942158 Day Mark, Chapel (remains of), Cairns, Field system

This exposed heather moorland is rich in archaeological remains. The red and white conical granite **daymark** for shipping (1), with its internal flight of stairs and blocked doorway was erected by Thomas Ekin in 1683. The inscribed date stone has been wrongly recut **1637** and should read **1687**.

Immediately below are the barely visible foundations of the small 8th-10th century

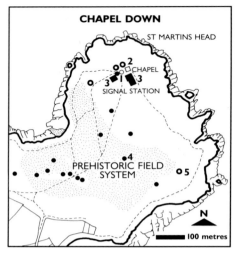

chapel (2) which gave its name to this part of St Martin's.

The **signal station** (3) was one of a series set up around the coast of Britain during the Napoleonic Wars to send information and orders to men-of-war waiting offshore (using a flag, pendant and four canvas balls). It was in use from 1810 until replaced by the semaphore tower on St Mary's [53] around 1814. A two-phased enclosure surrounds the main building, which accommodated four naval

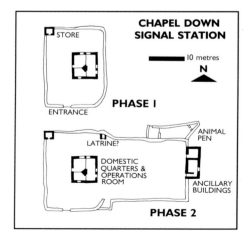

operators. Heavily robbed of stone, it still retains its central chimney breast. Several ancillary buildings are incorporated in the enclosure wall and an animal pen built against its east side. The signal post (an old ship's mast) probably stood to the north-east near the base of a more recent lookout. A small field to the west may also be associated.

A prehistoric rectilinear **field system** extends over most of Chapel Down. The boundaries are now low turf-covered stony banks, most obvious during early summer when they show as lines of yellow birdsfoot trefoil.

Cairns also survive. Simple mounds may represent stones cleared from the early fields, but others have a more ritual appearance, like the cairn (**4**) which has a **menhir** protruding from it forming one side of a possible cist grave.

The **entrance grave** (**5**) with partially kerbed mound and ruinous chamber has side slabs but no capstones. Set into the bedrock nearby and standing just 0.6 metres high is a carved piece of granite in the shape of a human head and shoulders. It was found re-used in a nearby early field wall during the 1940s. It has broken from a taller shaft and may be the top part of a **Romano-Celtic idol** or an earlier Bronze Age **statue menhir**.

29 CRUTHER'S HILL
Entrance graves and cairn
SV 929152 *Chambered Cairns*

On the north-western knoll is an **entrance grave** with a kerb of very large boulders and outcrop, and an off-centre chamber with walls but no capstones. Half-way along the ridge lies a second **entrance grave** with a kerb similar to the first and a chamber with its floor and walls of large boulders and natural rocks. No capstones remain. On the south-eastern knoll are an entrance grave and a **cairn**. The first has an oval mound with an incomplete stone kerb and a ruinous central chamber of boulders set on edge with two upright stones flanking its entrance but no capstones. The second is a circular cairn, partially kerbed with upright boulders and with an off-centre cist built against natural rock. Stone slabs form its other three sides, but no capstones survive.

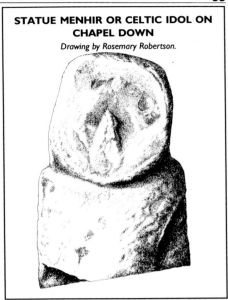

STATUE MENHIR OR CELTIC IDOL ON CHAPEL DOWN

Drawing by Rosemary Robertson.

30 ST MARTIN'S CHURCH
Church, cross base, sundial
SX 928156 *shown as church symbol*

St Martin's **church** was built around 1683 by Thomas Ekin, the Godolphins' Steward in the Islands, and repaired in 1820 by George Woodley (SPCK missionary minister for St Agnes and St Martin's). Woodley also extended the graveyard, a 'mere croft, surrounded by a low, tottering hedge', to create the present rectangular stone-walled enclosure. In 1866 after being struck by lightning the church was rebuilt by Augustus Smith. Evidence suggests that the present church is built on the site of an 11th-12th century chapel and graveyard, the focus of one of the medieval settlements on St Martin's. A socketed rectangular block of granite built into the church's east wall is probably a **medieval cross base** associated with the earlier establishment. Later is the square pillar just south of the south-west corner: the **base of a sundial** probably set up by Ekin.

31 TINKLER'S HILL KELP PIT
SX 916165

Close to the cliff edge at the foot of the eastern slope of Tinkler's Hill lies a good example of a kelp pit. Stone-lined, it is 1.5 metres in diameter and 0.5 metres deep.

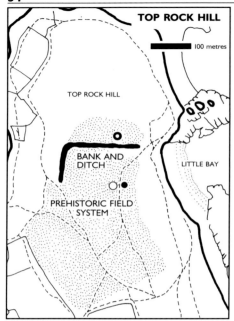

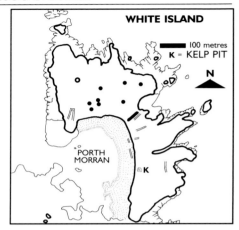

32 TOP ROCK HILL

Entrance grave, cairn, round house, field system, bank and ditch

SX 922167 *Cairns, Hut Circle, Cairn, Field system*

A possible entrance grave consists of a heather-covered mound with an open-ended box on its west side (formed by three slabs set on edge) probably the remains of a **chamber or cist**. A possible displaced capstone lies to the east. South are the disturbed remains of a circular platform **cairn**, with a rectangular depression (the result of antiquarian digging), adjoined by a large prehistoric field bank. The prehistoric **round house** is a levelled platform enclosed by a low circular bank. It abuts a low lynchet, part of a prehistoric **field system** of banks and lynchets forming a rectilinear

pattern, extending over 6 hectares but partly obscured by blown sand. Overlying this system is a substantial earth and sand **bank** of unknown date and function running east-west turning at its west end to run north-south. It measures about 10 metres wide and 2.5 metres high with traces of a ditch on the south.

33 WHITE ISLAND

Entrance grave, cairns, bank and ditch, field system, kelp pit

SV 924175 *Chambered Cairn, Cairns, Field System*

A well-preserved **entrance grave** consisting of a circular cairn surrounded by an incomplete kerb of large boulders with an infilled chamber, with coursed stone walls and two capstones still in place. On the slopes below lie nine small **cairns** (some kerbed). A low stony **bank** ditched on its south side cuts the island in half. Of unknown date, it is later in character than the fragmentary prehistoric **field system** of boulder walls, forming a rectilinear pattern. On the clifftop to the east of Porth Morran is a **kelp pit**.

Map of St Martin's, 1708, *redrawn by Charles Thomas*

ST MARY'S

34: Bant's Carn entrance grave

34 BANT'S CARN ENTRANCE GRAVE
SV 910123 *Bant's Carn*

The most famous of the Scillonian entrance graves, a very fine example, well maintained by English Heritage. Excavated in 1900 by George Bonsor, he found four piles of cremated bone at the far end of the chamber and sherds of pottery in the passage outside its entrance. Most of the pottery was typically Bronze Age but the most important find was part of a round-based neolithic bowl. In 1970, during the re-erection of a fallen capstone and door jamb, more Bronze Age pottery was recovered. Today visitors see an inner high-standing cairn, revetted by a kerb of coursed stone housing the chamber. Outside is a lower, **D**-shaped platform, retained by a boulder kerb, with an unroofed stone-lined passage giving access to the chamber entrance (an unusual feature). The boat-shaped chamber, of coursed walling roofed with four massive capstones, is much higher than most others. A substantial lynchet, part of a prehistoric field system, forms the mound's south-east side and a modern wall has been constructed over its south-western edge.

35 BUZZA HILL ENTRANCE GRAVE
SV 906104 *Chambered Cairn*

Commanding panoramic views, this large kerbed cairn is one of two entrance graves excavated on Buzza Hill during the mid-18th century by the Cornish antiquarian, William Borlase, who found neither pottery nor human bones. It has an off-centre chamber with no entrance. This may be a cist. The stone sealing its north-east end is possibly a fallen capstone. One large capstone remains in place.

36 BUZZA TOWER
SV 906104

Previously called *King Edward's Tower* this well known landmark has been maintained since 1912 as a memorial to the King's visit, but was originally a windmill built in 1834 to replace the earlier Peninnis Mill [50]. It stands on a kerbed platform which probably incorporates the remains of a Bronze Age cairn excavated by William Borlase during the 18th century.

37 CARN MORVAL BATTERY
SV 906119

This Civil War gun battery was designed to defend the entrance to St Mary's Pool. **V**-shaped in plan, with a field of fire to the north-west and south-west, it survives as low turf-covered banks. To the north is a sub-rectangular bivouac platform, cut into the natural slope, revetted on its downhill side by low coursed walling.

38 CASTLE ENNOR

SV 914103 *Castle (rems of)*

This castle, apparently built by one of the earls of Cornwall, is first mentioned in 1244. It is known to have been occupied in 1306, but licence to crenellate was not granted until 1315. Described as 'a meatley strong pile' by Leland in 1536, a 1554 account of ordnance says it was used as an armoury and fortified with five light guns to defend Old Town harbour and quay [**48**]. Castle Ennor was robbed of stone for the building of Star Castle [**54**] in 1593. All that remains is a single, obtuse-angled drystone wall, incorporating and revetting a semi-circular rock outcrop with a vertical face on its west side and a narrow flattish top.

This site is on private land and can only be viewed from a distance.

39 GIANT'S CASTLE CLIFF CASTLE

SV 925100 *Giant's Castle, fort*

Four curvilinear stone and earth banks cutting off the promontory from Salakee Down. There are traces of outer ditches, across which two staggered causeways join the 2nd, 3rd and 4th banks. There are no signs of habitation within the exposed interior. Excavation of the west end of the outer rampart prior to the construction of a World War Two lookout produced pottery dating to about 300 BC (Iron Age).

40 HALANGY DOWN SETTLEMENT AND FIELD SYSTEM

SV 910124 *Settlement, Field system*

The remains of an Iron Age and Romano-British **settlement** maintained by English Heritage. A complex of interconnecting stone built houses, which include simple oval structures (some with rectangular annexes) and a single courtyard house, a dwelling type characteristic of the Roman period in West Cornwall. Excavation of

40: Halangy Down settlement, with Bant's Carn entrance grave at top right

most of the settlement (during 1950 and 1964-71) revealed interesting internal features: stone-lined drains, hearths, post-holed stones, benches, partitions, sanded floors and small chambers, probably stores or cupboards, constructed within the thick walls, which sometimes overlaid earlier features, like corn-drying ovens. The buildings had been modified over 500 years, the courtyard house representing the last occupation phase, and probably housed successive generations of the same extended family. The settlement sits on a low cultivation terrace. On the hillside nearby are the remains of an extensive **field system**, and **round houses**, probably of Bronze Age date.

41 HARRY'S WALLS

Fort, menhir

SV 909109 *Battery*

An unfinished **fort** in the care of English Heritage. Though named Harry's Walls, it was begun in 1551, during the reign of Edward VI. An early plan (reproduced on the site information plaque) shows it was intended to be square with acutely angled bastions at each corner—an Italian design reflecting the increasing use of cannon. Internal buildings are depicted against the curtain wall on all four sides and a brewhouse and mill was to be erected next to a fresh water pool below the hill. Bad siting appears to have been the reason for completion of only the south-west side, visible as two bastions connected by a curtain wall heavily robbed of its dressed facing stones. A well-built drain passing through this wall shows where ground level would have been. A foundation trench indicates the proposed line of the north-western curtain wall. Outside stands a tall slender stone first recorded by Borlase in 1756 as sitting on a mound. Secured in position in recent years, this is probably a Bronze Age **menhir** in its original position, with traces of a surrounding cairn.

42 HUGH TOWN OLD QUAY
SV 902107

Still in use today, this impressive quay was originally built in 1601, following the construction of Star Castle [54] and the shift of settlement from Old Town to below the Hugh. Rebuilt in 1749-51, it survives apparently unchanged with large granite blocks placed vertically in unmortared courses. Augustus Smith's 19th century quay abuts it at right angles halfway along.

43 INNISIDGEN ENTRANCE GRAVES
SV 922127 *Chambered Cairn, Innisidgen Carn*

Two entrance graves—Innisidgen Carn and Lower Innisidgen—both maintained by English Heritage. **Innisidgen Carn** is in very good condition, with a substantial mound revetted by a kerb of coursed walling, and a partially infilled central chamber. Its walls are of slabs and coursed stone and it has five capstones. **Lower Innisidgen** is more ruinous. The

41: Harry's Walls from the air

mound incorporates outcrops, the kerb is incomplete and it has a trapezoidal chamber, with an original south entrance.

44 LONG ROCK
Menhir
SV 914124 *Long Rock Standing Stone*

This menhir is apparently in its original position. 2.4 metres high, the smooth-faced stone leans towards the south-east and tapers slightly at its top. Flint tools have been found nearby.

45 MOUNT TODDEN BATTERY
SV 929115 *Battery*

A large Civil War battery, named *old watch house* on Spence's 1792 map and described by Troutbeck (1796) as a sod battery of rose pattern. In his time an unmounted cannon remained and he noted that during war three islanders and one soldier kept a nightly lookout from the bomb-proof watch house. Today, the **battery** appears sub-square in plan, with

43: Lower Innisidgen entrance grave

44: Long Rock menhir *see previous page*

belongs to the last restoration. On the apex of the east end gable is one of the small granite crosses thought to have marked the limit of church land during Norman times. Prominent in the churchyard are memorials to Augustus Smith, and Louise Holzmaister, one of 328 passengers lost during the wreck of the *SS Schiller*, in 1875.

47 OLD TOWN FISH-SALTING TROUGH
SV 914102

47: Old Town fish salting trough ©*Frank Gibson*

On the east side of Old Town Bay is a deep rectangular trough cut from a single granite block. Troutbeck (1796) says it was used for salting, when all the fish of the Islands were brought here for curing and stages were erected in the adjoining field for drying fish in the sun. According to him, the trough will hold eighteen Winchester bushels and was dug from a quarry on Salakee Down. At both ends the trough's inner faces slope inward. Incisions in one of its outer corners may be associated with lifting tackle.

48 OLD TOWN QUAY
SV 914101 *Old Quay*

Visible at low water is a ruined quay first mentioned in 1554 in connection with the fortification of Castle Ennor [**38**], but probably old then. It may originally have been built at the same time as the 13th century castle. A sketch of 1756 depicts the quay as it is today; **L**-shaped in plan and tapering towards its seaward end. Of drystone construction, with vertically set facing stones retaining a core of large boulders, it has two building phases, but only the lower courses survive.

rounded corners and bowed sides, enclosed by an earth and stone bank. The western entrance is formed by a sharp inturn of the bank at the north-west corner. In the interior stands the **watch house**, with a natural boulder on one of its sides, the others of stone walling, and roofed, except on its south-west side, by massive granite lintels, over which is a turf-covered earth and stone mound. The entrance is on the south-west and traces of original openings can be seen in the top of this wall and that on the north-east. The demolished remains of a 20th century concrete building lie close by.

46 OLD TOWN CHURCH
SV 911100 *shown as church symbol*

Erected between 1130 and 1140AD, a north and south aisle were added during the 17th century. The church was rebuilt during the 1830s and restored in 1890. All that survives of the original Norman building is a round-headed arch leading to the present vestry porch. This may have originally divided the nave from a side chapel. The three-light stained glass window above the altar probably

49: Peninnis Head battery (the platform between the two outcrops) with the lighthouse in the background

49 PENINNIS HEAD BATTERY
SV 911094 Batteries

The substantial remains of a Civil War battery. Troutbeck noted (1796) that guns were placed here in Queen Anne's reign (1702-14) and a parish account for the remaking of fences torn down to make a passage for them. Lying between two outcrops, the battery consists of a sub-rectangular platform with a projecting point to the south enclosed by an earthen bank up to a metre high. Though the bank is now breached on the north-west and south-east sides, the original entrance was probably on the north-east.

50 PENINNIS MILL
SV 910097 *marked but not named*

A ruined windmill, built by Francis Godolphin in 1726 when it became difficult for civilians to use those within The Garrison [54]. By Troutbeck's time (1796) it was the only grist mill on the island, but was in poor shape and corn had to be sent to Cornwall for milling. By 1798 it was working again with Robert Maybee as the miller, and continued in use until 1834 when superseded by Buzza Tower [36]. The disused mill later served as a signal tower and when Listed in 1954, it stood 3.7 metres high. Demolished in 1960, all that remains is its granite base, housing the lower millstone and bearing a date stone, **FG 1726** and another inscribed **WT**.

51 PORTH HELLICK DOWN
Entrance graves and cairns
SV 928107 *Chambered Cairn (2)*

A group of seven entrance graves and two cairns. Slightly distanced from the main group is the largest and most impressive entrance grave (1), heavily restored and now maintained

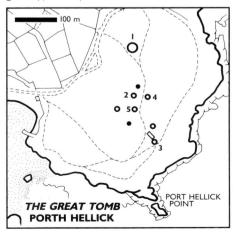

by English Heritage. It was called *The Great Tomb* by George Bonsor, during excavations in 1899 which involved exposing the capstones, the inner kerb, and examining the chamber contents. The latter had already been destroyed, leaving only a piece of pumice and a few Bronze Age potsherds. An outer stone kerb recorded by Bonsor was removed and the inner kerb modified during restoration. The monument consists of a large platformed cairn retained by a kerb of coursed walling housing a chamber, with four massive capstones and an entrance constricted by a projecting jambstone (an uncommon feature), with an unroofed passage giving access to it (also unusual). The line of the former kerb is visible as a low bank 2.7 metres out from the inner kerb.

Unrestored, but easily recognisable, are four of the other six **entrance graves**, each with their chamber sides and at least one capstone surviving. (**2**) and (**3**) are very ruinous so that chambers are mere central depressions. Entrance graves (**4**) and (**5**) were excavated by Reverend Woodley around 1822. The **cairns**, very low circular platforms, are harder to detect.

52 SIR CLOUDESLEY SHOVEL'S GRAVE
SV 926107

At the top of the beach on the west side of Porth Hellick is a small monument to Sir Cloudesley Shovel of the *HMS Association*, flagship of the fleet wrecked on the Gilstone Ledges in 1707. A roughly-cut upright stone block on a pedestal marks the spot where his body was temporarily buried after being washed ashore. He was later reinterred in Westminster Abbey.

53 TELEGRAPH TOWER
SV 912121 *Coastguard*

This circular granite building was erected on the highest point of the Islands as a gun and semaphore tower soon after 1805. Later adapted as a signal station, it was here, in 1898, that Guglielmo Marconi heard wireless signals transmitted from Porthcurno (thirty miles away in West Cornwall). The four-storeyed building, 12.0 metres high, serves as the Coastguard headquarters and weather reporting station.

54 THE GARRISON
SV 898103 *see insert map opposite*

This heavily defended headland, originally known as The Hugh, provides visible evidence of the main episodes in Scilly's military history from the late-16th to the mid-20th century.

The earliest fortification is **Star Castle**, built for Elizabeth I by Francis Godolphin in 1593. The shape of an eight-pointed star, the castle is entered by a short flight of steps across a small stone bridge over a dry moat and through a projecting gatehouse with a portcullis recess and inscribed **ER 1593**. Inside, the thick curtain wall with blocked gunports is divided from the taller inner building by a narrow passageway. This building originally had a basement for storage, two floors for accommodation of the garrison and an attic. Guardhouses stand on top of the curtain, with a bellcote—an 18th century addition like the lead cisterns now outside St Mary's Church and the stone-lined

54 The Elizabethan defences—Star Castle (top right) and the curtain wall across the neck (left of centre)

dewpond or beacon pit visible south of the castle. Star Castle served as a prison as well as a fortress, but is now an hotel.

Around 1600 a stretch of **curtain wall** was constructed across the neck of The Hugh. The curtain survives (from Jeffersons (1)) to Lower Benham Battery (2) as an uncoursed rubble wall, but all the batteries visible along its line are later additions or rebuilds, as is the main gateway. There were originally three **sally ports**; one (3) is still in use, another (4) has been blocked but its portcullis slot can still be seen and a third (5) now forms the private access to a garden. A deep rock-cut ditch along the eastern side of the curtain wall is silted up, but still visible in places.

During the Civil War (1642-46) Royalists erected **breastwork** around The Hugh,

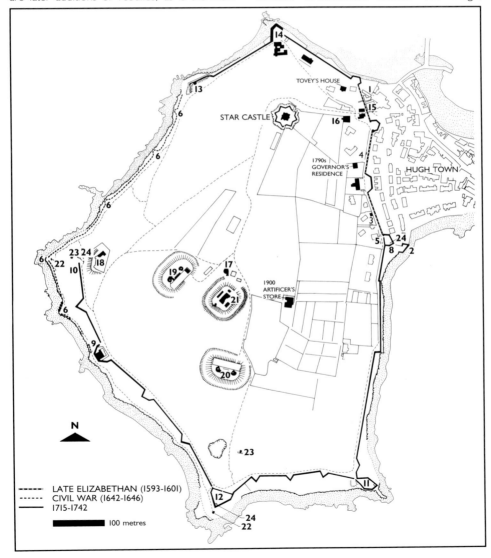

TOVEY'S HOUSE

STAR CASTLE

1790s GOVERNOR'S RESIDENCE

HUGH TOWN

1900 ARTIFICER'S STORE

N

LATE ELIZABETHAN (1593-1601)
CIVIL WAR (1642-1646)
1715-1742

100 metres

54: Civil War breastwork on The Garrison

except across the neck where it was already defended by curtain wall. Much was replaced by the 18th century fortifications but parts are still visible on the cliff edge on the headland's west and north-west sides as a low turf-covered bank with shallow inner ditch incorporating several small bastions for guns (6).

Between 1715 and 1746 The Hugh attained its formidably defended character and became known as The Garrison. The **curtain wall** was rebuilt and extended around most of the headland; in 1715-42 from Benham (8) to the un-named battery (9) (where there is a 4.0 metre gap in the wall) and in 1742-46 from here to Steval Point (10). This last stretch is constructed of massive smooth-faced ashlar blocks with thin mortar joins and contrasts with the earlier 18th century wall built of smaller coursed stones. A stub of wall attached to its northern end (10) represents the remains of a small single-storey building used as a guard-droom and prison. The curtain wall, capable of mounting 120 guns, has embrasures on its top and drainage channels at its base. The sea approaches were covered by **batteries** in large bastions, principally at Morning Point (11), Woolpack Point (12) and south of Steval Point (9). Between these, redans increased flanking fire. Charles' Battery (13) and Newman's Platform (14) covered the north side. The present Garrison Gate (15) is a modification of the late Elizabethan structure, having an 18th century bellcote and parapet. Inscribed stones read **GR 1742 FG** and **AT** for King George, Francis Godolphin and Abraham Tovey. Also rebuilt at this time was the **magazine** (16), a sunken building surrounded by a massive blast

wall, known as the Rocket House. Interesting features include ventilation ports and hand-carved granite ridge stones.

Little change occurred until 1834 when an old **windmill** on top of The Garrison was rebuilt as a **gun tower** (17), later (1900) used as a signal station.

In the 1890s Scilly was classed as a defended port and an advanced signal station. Over the next fifteen years four **batteries** (18-20) were built to withstand attacks from enemy cruisers and torpedo-boats. Woolpack (20) and Steval (19) batteries each had 2 x 6 inch Quick fire guns. Between them was a defensible **barracks** (21). Associated **searchlights** (22) and **operations huts** (23) were built at Woolpack and Steval points, with an engine room on the Garrison Walls (9). Steval Point (18) and Bant's Carn Battery had 2 x 12 pounder Quick Fire guns. All were dismantled by 1906. Only Woolpack can be visited.

During both World Wars The Garrison accommodated hundreds of servicemen and the remains of World War II concrete **machine gun posts** (24) still stand.

54: The old windmill reused as a signal station

55 TOLL'S ISLAND

Field system, breastwork, battery, kelp pits, quay
SV 931119 *Pellew's Redoubt*

Reached via a sandbar at low tide, this small island boasts a variety of archaeological remains. A fragmentary **prehistoric field system** survives on the south slope, where rough boulder alignments form a rectilinear pattern. Other walls were probably robbed for the Civil War defences. The lengths of **breastwork** survive as a low turf-covered bank with traces of an inner ditch. One is attached to a kidney-shaped **battery**, known as Pellew's Redoubt, occupying the island's highest point. Two half bastions, placed back to back, command a wide field of fire. The raised interior is enclosed by a stone and earth rampart, with an entrance on the west revetted on one side with stone slabs. Quarry pits are visible outside the battery. Four **kelp pits** are strung along the cliff edge on the south side of Toll's Island. Off its south-western corner, below high water, are the remains of a slightly curving **quay**, with a core of granite boulders retained by 2-3 courses of facing stones, terminating in a massive boulder topped by an iron ring.

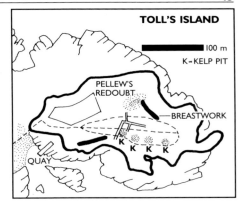

56 TOLL'S PORTH

Battery, breastwork, kelp pit
SV 908123 *Battery*

An overgrown flat-topped sandy mound at the north end of Toll's Porth appears to be the remains of a Civil War **battery**, recorded by Troutbeck (1796). A length of **breastwork** runs for 50 metres along the cliff edge on the porth's south side. It consists of a stone and earth bank with a stone revetment on the seaward side exposed by coastal erosion. The footpath follows the line of an inner ditch and to the south lies a good example of a **kelp pit**.

SAMSON

57 NECK OF SAMSON

Cottage, well
SV 878127 *the well is marked*

The **ruined post-medieval cottage** was excavated in 1976. Its clay-mortared walls were built directly onto sand, with no foundation trench. Single-storeyed, it has a doorway and window in its south wall. Excavation revealed a clay floor replacing an earlier sand one, fragments of glass indicating that the window was glazed, and an absence of slate suggesting a thatched roof. Internal features include a threshold stone, large inglenook fireplace, cupboard recess and ledge for a half loft or rafters. A limpet midden was excavated a few metres from the doorway. Unmarked on a map of 1829-33, this cottage appears to have been occupied between 1833 and 1855. Below South Hill is an oval stone-lined **well** (choked with sand and only a metre deep) in use during post-medieval times.

57: Samson cottages at the turn of the century
© Frank Gibson

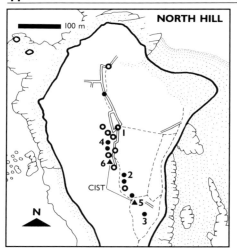

58 NORTH HILL
Entrance graves, cairns, cists, field system
SV 877131 *Chambered Cairns*

The hilltop is dominated by a linear group of Bronze Age burial monuments, connected by prehistoric field boundaries. Of the **entrance graves** the best example (1) is a substantial cairn, revetted by kerbstones, contains a well-preserved chamber, of slightly corbelled drystone walling roofed by two capstones. Hencken's 1930 excavation found no human remains but flints, a possible whetstone, neolithic pottery and several pebbles lying around the chamber entrance. Floor paving beneath the surviving capstones incorporated a re-used saddle quern. Four abutting field banks apparently post-date this monument.

Of the other **cairns**, (2) consists only of a stone kerb and may be a ring cairn, the central depression in (3) is probably due to antiquarian digging. When cairn (4) was excavated by Augustus Smith in 1862, a small cist grave was found with side slabs having flush-tenon joints filled with clay mortar. The floor was paved and cremated bone was found in one corner. The single capstone is now displaced and the interior partially infilled. The height of the cairn has been raised by excavated material dumped on top

of it. An unexplained find was a bronze statuette which Smith considered to be Romano-British.

Two other **cists** on North Hill have no covering cairn. Cist (5) is rectangular, with sides of larger stones packed with smaller ones and a displaced capstone. Cist (6) is polygonal, with two large capstones.

The prehistoric boulder walls and banks form a fragmentary rectilinear pattern and are probably part of the same **field system** as those surviving on Samson flats and South Hill [60].

59 SAMSON FLATS FIELD SYSTEM
SV 880128

On the tidal flats are the remains of a prehistoric field system — seaweed-covered boulder walls spread by wave action. They are best viewed from the top of North or South Hill, where surviving boundaries as well as one on the tiny Puffin Island are probably part of the same large system.

60 SOUTH HILL
Entrance graves, round houses, field system, cottages, barns, well, deerpark
SV 878124 *Cairns, Hut circles*

On the highest part of this hill, on a natural granite platform, lies a linear arrangement of four impressive **entrance graves**. At the north end a large oval cairn, revetted by closely set kerbstones (two courses high) contains a chamber formed by five slabs, with two possible displaced capstones. An unusual entrance grave to the south is really two in

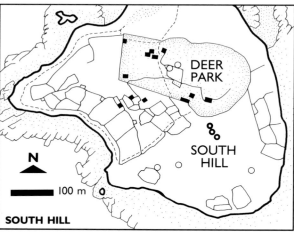

60: One of the South Hill entrance graves

one. Two well-preserved chambers share a single irregular cairn, kerbed on all sides except the south-west where the kerb connects with the wall of one of the chambers. Further south a cairn piled against the east face of the rock outcrop has a chamber with a large capstone at its north end and a prehistoric wall abutting its north-east side.

Two-thirds of the enclosures covering the slopes of South Hill are of prehistoric origin. Lynchets, boulder walls and stony banks form a patchwork of little **fields**. Amongst these five **round houses** survive as circular or oval platforms levelled into the hillslope, enclosed on their downhill side by low walling.

More obvious are the remains of much later settlement, the stark ruined **cottages and barns** of the post-medieval period. Most houses are simple dwellings (some originally having timber lofts) constructed of clay-mortared rubble walling. Around some are limpet shells, the remains of kitchen middens, and at the foot of a rock face on the north side of the hill is a shallow well. Drystone walls form an associated **field system**, rectilinear in pattern, but more irregular where the walls overlie prehistoric boundaries. The population

peaked around 1829, nine cottages housing thirty-seven people. Following the depopulation of Samson in 1855, Augustus Smith enclosed 3.5 hectares on the northern slopes of South Hill with a substantial stone-wall to create a **deerpark**. By 1860 the experiment had failed, deer apparently escaping across the flats to Tresco. The impressive entrance to the park is on its north side, the main footpath up South Hill passing through it.

Between mid-April and mid-July birds nest beneath the bracken on the southern and south-western sides of this hill and visitors are requested to avoid these slopes.

TEAN

Between 15th April and 20th July visitors to Tean are asked to take special care to avoid disturbing ringed plovers and terns nesting at the top of the beach.

61 GREAT HILL
Entrance graves, cairn/round house
SV 909166 *Chambered Cairns*

On the summit of this hill, built against an outcrop, is a flat-topped cairn surrounded by ten kerbstones housing a rectangular **chamber**, whose walls protrude just above ground level. No capstones survive. To the south, an oval area enclosed by a low stone and earth wall is either a **ring cairn or round house**, with a possible entrance on its south side. At the hill's south-western end, a cairn, defined by a kerb of massive slabs (now mostly fallen) and natural rocks, contains a **chamber**, with slab and coursed walling, partly destroyed on the south-east side. There are two displaced capstones.

62 WEST PORTH
Field system, cairn
SV 907163 *Cairn (submerged)*

Visible below high water mark is a fragmentary system of rectilinear **fields** defined by boulder walls. Some are well-preserved with long stretches of set boulders, others have become spread by wave action. They are of prehistoric or Romano-British date and probably originally connected with similar ones on Old Man, in East Porth and in and around St Helen's Porth. On the south-west side of the system is a large **cairn**, stones heaped around natural rock with seven possible kerbstones around its perimeter — the result of stone clearance or a burial cairn.

63 WEST SIDE OF EAST PORTH
Settlement, chapel and cemetery
SV 908164 *Chapel (remains of)*

An important multi-period domestic and ecclesiastical site excavated by Charles Thomas in 1956. It consisted of a Romano-British (1st-4th century) midden; an early medieval (6th-7th century) sub-rectangular hut and cemetery of 16 stone-lined cist graves; an early 8th century stone chapel dedicated to St Theona; late 12th or 13th century occupation; documentary evidence for a house ruined by 1652; a stone house said to have been built in the late 17th century by the Nance family who brought the kelp industry to Scilly and lived on Tean for several generations; and a late 18th century farmstead. The **midden** can still be seen on the low clifftop to the west, but the early medieval hut is no longer visible. One of the **graves** was thought to be that of the religious founder (St Theona). Other skeletons showed signs of leprosy and this, together with imported pottery, suggested that Christianity was introduced to Scilly from the Mediterranean or Middle East. Most of the cemetery was backfilled, but graves 1 and 9 remain uncovered. **St Theona's chapel** is a small rectangular building aligned east-west, with

62: West Porth field walls and cairn (centre top)

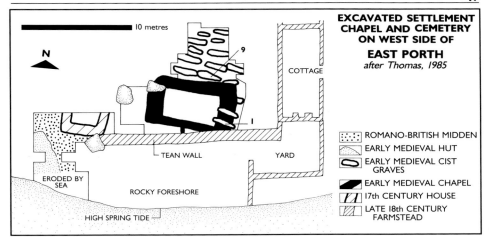

10 metres

N

COTTAGE

TEAN WALL

YARD

ERODED BY SEA

ROCKY FORESHORE

HIGH SPRING TIDE

ROMANO-BRITISH MIDDEN
EARLY MEDIEVAL HUT
EARLY MEDIEVAL CIST GRAVES
EARLY MEDIEVAL CHAPEL
17th CENTURY HOUSE
LATE 18th CENTURY FARMSTEAD

traces of a south doorway. Excavation spoil obscures the north wall; the eastern was removed during excavation. The **17th century house**, occupied throughout the 18th century, was only partially excavated and subsequently buried by excavation rubble, with only a metre of its south end now visible. The **late 18th century farmhouse** stands mostly to roof level, with a doorway in the centre of the east wall and a fireplace at the south end, flanked by a cupboard recess and a window. A ruined **outbuilding** stands to the north and a yard to the south and a **wall**, known as Tean Wall extends from the south-west corner.

Associated with this, or an earlier phase to the south-east is a ruined **quay** comprising two parallel lines of boulders running down the beach.

TRESCO

64 APPLETREE BAY
Field system, enclosure
SV 891135 *Field walls shown but not named*
At and below mean low tide are the remains of a prehistoric **field system** and a post-medieval enclosure. The former consists of four lengths of boulder wall, (periodically obscured by shifting sand) best viewed from the top of the dune or Oliver's Battery [72]. The longest wall is only accessible at low spring tide, as is the small rectangular **enclosure** formed of closely placed boulders, well-faced on the inside but rough on the outside. In the absence of an entrance, this may be a post-medieval oyster bed.

65 BATHINGHOUSE PORTH
Round houses, field system
SV 894135 *marked but not named*
Boulder walls form a rectilinear prehistoric

field system extending from the top of the beach into the intertidal zone. Two possible **round houses** have been identified, (1) consists only of a curved section of wall and (2) lies, difficult to detect, amongst a mass of boulders. These remains are periodically obscured by sand.

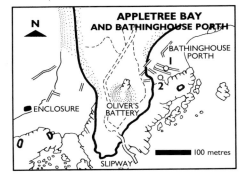

APPLETREE BAY
AND BATHINGHOUSE PORTH

N

BATHINGHOUSE PORTH

OLIVER'S BATTERY

ENCLOSURE

SLIPWAY

100 metres

66 BEACON HILL LOOKOUT

SV 888157

South-east of the triangulation point is a rectangular platform on which stand the remains of a building, probably the ruined lookout recorded by Troutbeck (1796). Additional walls extending from the south-west side are of unknown function.

67 BLOCKHOUSE

SV 897155 *Blockhouse*

This blockhouse is maintained by English Heritage. Constructed in 1554, it replaced a smaller earlier one and consists of a rectangular paved platform high on a natural carn, reached by stone steps. Its enclosing walls originally had a parapet, with embrasures at the western ends of the north and south sides. Meagre living quarters were provided by a lean-to in the south-west corner, lit by a window in the west wall, subsequently blocked. A rectangular recess in the south wall has a door rebate and a stone corbelled roof and may have been a powder or ammunition locker. Another blocked recess is visible near the block-house entrance. At a later period a living room with two small windows and a fireplace was added against the south-west corner. Little is known about the use of the blockhouse from its erection until the Civil War, when it was used by Royalists in their un-successful defence of Tresco. The 1652 Parliamentary survey calls it *Dover Fort*. A **U**-shaped turf-covered bank sur-rounding the south and west sides of the flat-topped knoll may date from the Civil War. Two banks lower down the slope, inundated by blown sand, are of un-known date.

68 CASTLE DOWN

King Charles' Castle and earthwork, fortification, battery, breastwork, tin mining, enclosures, cairns, entrance graves, field system, round houses

SV 885160 *Castle (rems of), Earthwork (2), Battery (rem of) Cairns, Chambered Cairns, Settlement and Field System*

An extensive area of heather moorland rich in prehistoric and post-medieval remains.

Maintained by English Heritage, **King Charles' Castle** was probably built between 1550 and 1554, when it was equipped with artillery. It is subdivided, with the armament massed on the western side to cover the entrance to New Grimsby Harbour and the garrison's domestic quarters on the east. Semi-hexagonal in plan to provide a wide field of fire, the western end was originally two-storeyed to accommodate at least two tiers of guns. The five ground floor gunports survive, with patches of the paved gun

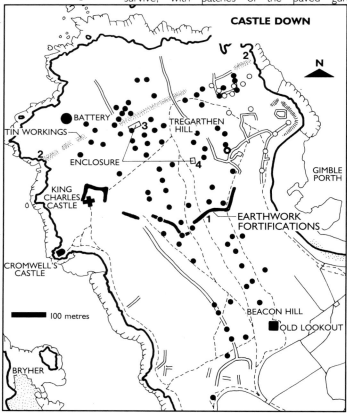

CASTLE DOWN

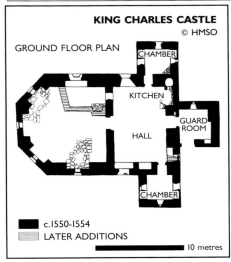

KING CHARLES CASTLE
© HMSO

GROUND FLOOR PLAN

CHAMBER

KITCHEN

GUARD ROOM

HALL

CHAMBER

■ c.1550-1554
▨ LATER ADDITIONS

10 metres

platforms behind. Two upper gunports, with a greater external splay, have been reconstructed in the south-east corner. The cruciform domestic range, lit by small internally splayed windows, consists of a hall, with a kitchen at its north end probably partitioned off by a wooden screen. The large kitchen fireplace incorporates a bread oven. Two smaller chambers north and south of the main room were probably sleeping quarters. The castle's main entrance has a four-centred arch (in common with the internal doorways) and a drawbar hole. Beyond is a guardroom. Later another living chamber of irregular shape was created in the north-east corner of the gun room. During the Civil War an irregular **bastioned earthwork**, consisting of a bank and outer ditch with an entrance on the south, was constructed on the castle's east side to protect it from landward attack. Badly sited, the castle's active life was short and it was heavily robbed for the building of its successor, Cromwell's Castle [69].

A very low **fortification** (1) extends from near King Charles' Castle to the eastern side of the Down. Consisting of a 0.2 metre high bank with an occasional shallow outer ditch, it incorporates a massive south facing bastion (with orillons) in its centre and a half bastion at its east end. There are traces of another unfinished bastion to the west. The shape of

these bastions indicates a 1550s date and this was probably an outwork to King Charles' Castle.

The probable remains of a Civil War **battery**, which gave rise to the local names *Gun well*, *Gun Hill* and *Gun Hole*, consists of a crescent-shaped bank with a sub-rectangular rock-cut hole on its landward side. A **breast-work** of similar date surrounds the small headland on the north-west of Gimble Porth. Its construction varies from a wall of spaced orthostats, infilled in places with earth and small stones, to a stone and earth bank embedded with recumbent boulders. At its south end it is overlaid by more recent walling. Towards the north end of Castle Down are the only remains of **tin mining** recorded in Scilly, probably the result of an abortive venture during the 1640s. Twenty-six small oval or sub-rectangular prospecting and extraction pits lie in a broad band along a north-east to south-west lode. A bow-shaped dam may be evidence for streamworking. Openworks (2) survive as narrow trenches dug from the cliff edge.

Close to the tinworkings and possibly associated with them is a **rectangular enclosure** (3) of unknown date and function. Its raised interior is surrounded by a stony bank and a shallow outer ditch, with no visible entrance. A poorly defined circular mound located at the south-west end of the enclosure may be the top of a Bronze Age cairn. On the south-west side of Tregarthen Hill is another enclosure (4) of uncertain date. Sub-rectangular and levelled into the slope, it is surrounded by a low bank with an internal ditch and no visible entrance. This may be the **site of a temporary building** erected between the 16th and 19th centuries.

Seventy-eight **cairns** survive on Castle Down. Most are low platforms or mounds, a third are partially surrounded by kerbs and one has a possible central cist. Some may be the result of stone clearance rather than burial.

On the south slope of Tregarthen Hill is an **entrance grave** consisting of a prominent cairn with an inner kerb of 11 stones and traces of an outer one. A chamber, built of coursed and slab walling, has two remaining capstones and was probably entered from the west. The

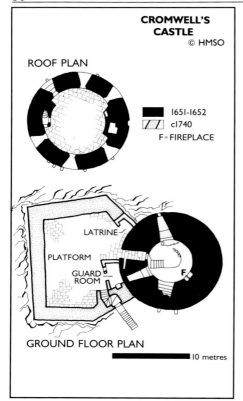

CROMWELL'S CASTLE
© HMSO

ROOF PLAN

■ 1651-1652
▨ c1740
F = FIREPLACE

LATRINE

PLATFORM

GUARD
ROOM

F

GROUND FLOOR PLAN

10 metres

cairns to the north and south each have a single kerb and a shallow depression, possibly a very ruined chamber.

Fragmentary Prehistoric **field systems** of boulder walls, banks and lynchets survive, robbed for the later military works on Castle Down. A linear earthwork on the south-west appears to form the eastern extent of one system and the long wall running from the south of Tregarthen Hill to the north coast may mark the western extent of another (though a single length of field wall has been identified further west).

There are two groups of **round houses** associated with these early fields. Four houses, strung along the north-west of Gimble Porth, consist of platforms cut back into or built out from the natural slope — enclosed by low walling. Two houses have annexes attached to their entrances, and one has a **D**-shaped platform perhaps a garden plot. The round

houses on the north side of Tregarthen Hill are of similar construction but generally smaller and of simple circular, oval or **D**-shaped plan.

69 CROMWELL'S CASTLE
SV 882159 *Castle*

Now in the care of English Heritage, this castle was named after Oliver Cromwell, and built in 1651-2, when the newly-captured Islands were threatened by the Dutch fleet. Erected on the site of a 16th century blockhouse, it superseded King Charles' Castle [68] in the defence of New Grimsby Harbour. A tall round tower was constructed of rubble in a style typical of the 16th and 17th century, similar to the outer wall of Star Castle on St Mary's [54]. Stone corbels projecting from the doorway high up in the tower's south side originally supported an external wooden platform reached by a staircase. A flight of intact stone steps led down from the doorway to the first floor. Inside, the loss of original timber floors and stairs (their positions marked by beam and joist holes and fireplaces) exposes the unlit basement and fine ribbed stone vault. In between these were two comfortable living storeys. A spiral stair within the tower wall leads up to the open platform, where six gunports pierce the massive walls, their splays characteristic of the mid-17th century. The paved platform was originally surrounded by a parapet. A few steps still lead up to the wall-head.

On the seaward side of the tower a battery for six guns was replaced by Abraham Tovey in the mid-18th century with a paved platform and low parapet. The tower's original doorway became a window, entry being via a new doorway cut through from the platform, which was reached by a flight of stone steps. A guardroom and a latrine were later built either side of the entrance. A small field visible on the hillslope to the east was probably used by soldiers garrisoned here or at King Charles' Castle.

70 MIDDLE DOWN MILL
SV 895152

Partially obscured by vegetation on the north side of the Down is the bottom stone of a horse-driven mill, carved out of natural rock. A circular platform with a central hole is surrounded by a channel, the outer rim of which has a small oval hole cut into it. Outside

70: Middle Down millstone

is a second channel, with the suggestion of a lip connecting it with the inner one. The top stone has been built into a wall elsewhere on Tresco. The mill is said to have been surrounded by a circle of stones at one time. It is of post-medieval character and was mentioned by Troutbeck (1796), but its function is uncertain; suggestions range from a cider press to a corn or even a tin mill. More likely, because of its isolated position and the lack of associated buildings, it was used to crush gorse for horse feed.

71 OLIVER'S BATTERY
SV 893135 *Oliver's Battery*

Commanding spectacular views, this is the only Parliamentarian battery in Scilly, built by Admiral Blake after the capture of Tresco (18th April 1651) and before the fall of St Mary's (23rd May). After an inauspicious start when one of its two guns exploded killing the gunner and an ensign, together with Blake's ships it pounded the Garrison until the Royalists surrendered.

On top of a small hill, to the south of a prominent granite outcrop, a pentagonal area is enclosed by a heather-covered bank with a shallow ditch on the west and south sides (on the east the natural slope is steep and the north is protected by a vertical rock face). The gun platform is in the south-east corner and a rectangular depression on the north may be the base of a building, perhaps a magazine or shelter. To the south a linear hollow may be an outer ditch or a natural feature formed by blown sand. Although the battery is 17th century, Bronze Age pottery collected from eroded parts of its bank suggests that it is on the site of an entrance grave.

72 TRESCO ABBEY GARDENS
Priory church, inscribed stone, holed stone, altar, brazier
SV 893143 *Priory*

Shrouded in exotic plants on the east side of the gardens are the ruins of a **Benedictine priory**, dedicated to St Nicholas, first mentioned in a grant of 1120, but already well established by then. There were probably only two or three brethren, with servants living close by and farming adjoining land. Hardly referred to beyond the 15th century, the priory was probably abandoned (because of attacks by pirates and raiders) before the Reformation. The only standing remains are the chancel and nave of the priory church, which appear little changed since they were sketched by Borlase in 1756, but were partially rebuilt during the last two centuries. There are two pointed arches in the south wall, the largest a crossing to the south transept of the church, the smaller a doorway leading into the north walk of the cloisters. In the centre of the north wall a blocked archway must have given access to the north transept. Opposing blocked windows are visible towards the east end of the church, and in the west wall is the south side of a blocked doorway, the walling to the north having

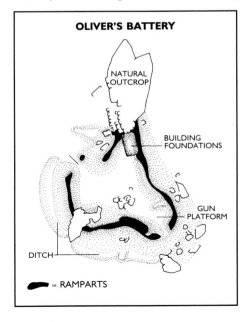

OLIVER'S BATTERY

NATURAL OUTCROP

BUILDING FOUNDATIONS

GUN PLATFORM

DITCH

⬛ = RAMPARTS

72: Inscribed tombstone

apparently been rebuilt. Part of a font base, decorated with round-arched arcading, was found inside the building. Most of the dressed stone used in the church was imported and some was re-used to kerb 18th century graves and later flowerbeds in its interior.

A 6th century **inscribed stone** has been re-used as a threshold stone for the south doorway. Broken in the past, it was originally part of an upright pillar, possibly associated with stone-lined graves found in a corner of the gardens. Its surface has become very worn, but it is just possible to make out part of a Latin inscription, **... THI FILI... COGI**, the last element being uncertain and perhaps reading instead **COGVI**, **COCI** or **COLINI** (the first I inscribed sideways). Whatever the reading, this is a standard formula meaning X, son of Y, with Latinised British personal names before and after **FILI**.

A short distance north-west of the priory church, bordering the path, is an upright granite pillar pierced by two holes. Tradition has it that a couple could become betrothed by holding hands through these. This probably represents later re-use of what may be a Bronze Age **holed stone**, a class of ritual monument contemporary with menhirs, stone circles and stone rows. Not in its original position, this appears to have been brought from Bryher.

At the west end of the Long Walk stands a **Roman altar**, the only one west of the River Tamar. It was found on St Mary's last century in a well below The Garrison, and brought to Tresco by Augustus Smith. A frontal panel for an inscription is blank, suggesting the dedication was painted or the altar was never dedicated. Most striking are the side panels depicting (in relief) a cleaver and a long-shafted axe, both probably sacrificial instruments. The stones cemented to the top and base of the altar were added for effect when it became a garden ornament.

In front of the Valhalla figurehead museum is an **iron brazier** or **cresset** from St Agnes Lighthouse [1], where a coal fire provided the light for a 110 years until replaced in 1790 by oil lamps with reflectors. This cresset (standing upside-down) was in use at the time of the conversion and must have been preceded by several others burnt out by the annual consumption of 107 tons of coal.

72: Brazier from St Agnes Lighthouse, now in Tresco Abbey Gardens

ISBN 0906294 28 2   © Cornwall Archaeological Unit 1992, 1995
First published 1992. Second impression, with minor amendments, 1995.
Twelveheads Press, Chy Mengleth, Twelveheads, Truro, Cornwall TR4 8SN